The creative screenwriter

Exercises to expand your craft

Zara Waldeback
and Craig Batty

2024

Methuen Dram

Methuen Drama

1 3 5 7 9 10 8 6 4 2

First published in 2012

Methuen Drama, an imprint of Bloomsbury Publishing Plc

Methuen Drama
Bloomsbury Publishing Plc
50 Bedford Square
London WC1B 3DP
www.methuendrama.com

Copyright © Zara Waldeback and Craig Batty 2012

Zara Waldeback and Craig Batty have asserted their rights under
the Copyright, Designs and Patents Act, 1988, to be identified
as the authors of this work

PB ISBN: 978 1 408 13719 2
E PUB ISBN: 978 1 408 15520 2

A CIP catalogue record for this book is available from the British Library

Available in the USA from Bloomsbury Academic & Professional,
175 Fifth Avenue/3rd Floor, New York, NY 10010
www.BloomsburyAcademicUSA.com

Designed and typeset by Country Setting, Kingsdown, Kent CT14 8ES
Printed and bound in Great Britain by CPI Group (UK) Ltd, Croydon CR0 4YY

Contents

Acknowledgements   2

Introduction   3

1   Being creative   7
What does creativity mean to you?   8
Ready, steady, go!   9
Limiting yourself   9
Magic moments   10
Wordplay   11
ABC stories   12
Spontaneous storytelling   12
Listening to an onion   13
Having fun!   14
Being bad   15

2   Generating ideas   16
Going to the heart   17
Finding the plot, finding the emotion   17
Into the unknown   18
What's around you?   19
Creative collisions   20
Bringing people together   21
What do you know? What don't you know?   22
Words of wisdom   23
Trading places   23
In the news   24
The hardest choice   25
Perfect fit   26

3   Developing stories   28
Growing up   29
Finding your compass   30

Assessing story potential   31
What's the problem?   32
Dot to dot   33
Conflict vs meaningful conflict   34
What happens next?   35
One thing leads to another   37
Back to the future   38
Losing the plot   39

4   Understanding characters   40

Pinpointing the protagonist   41
Supermarket sweep   43
Character building   43
A creative portrait   45
Inside out   46
What's in a name?   48
Stepping into change   49
Lost baggage   51
Motivating action   52
Public and private spheres   54

5   Shaping relationships   55

The odd couple   56
Finding the right antagonist   57
Antagonist as thematic driver   58
The third party   59
Weaving webs   61
Family values   62
A matter of perspective   63
Generating perspective   64
Listening out for relationships   65
Ensembles   66
Absent friends   67

6   Designing structure   68

Structuring the emotional journey   69
Character arc as structure   70
Chain reaction   71

Inciting incidents   71
All change   73
Planning the plan   73
Deepening the problem   75
Rising action   76
Making things worse   77
Plants and payoffs   78
Tying-up loose ends   79

7   Reimagining structure   81

Alternative routes   81
Where are you going?   83
Multiple protagonists   84
Parallel stories   85
Mix it up   86
Flashing back   88
Telling the time   89
Shapeshifting   90

8   Defining beginnings and endings   92

Starting over   93
Setting the dramatic question   93
Image is everything   94
First impressions   95
Pain and problems   96
Essential facts   96
Opening with voiceover   97
Full stop   98
Last dance   100
Mirror, mirror   100
One step beyond   101
Damp squib   102

9   Weaving worlds   103

Reframing the familiar   104
Beyond the sea   105
Television set   106
Outside the comfort zone   107

A whole new world   107
Playing by the rules   109
Opening doors   110
Bricks and mortar   111
When are we?   112
Inner worlds   113
A common language   114
Location, location, location   115

10 Exploring genre and form   117

Themes and dreams   118
Genre protagonists   119
Home sweet home   120
Fitting the bill   121
Mix and match   122
Setting the mood   123
It's no joke   124
Finding form   126

11 Enhancing scene writing   127

Fulfilling the function   128
The telling moment   129
The deciding factor   129
Scene structure   130
Turn up the heat   131
Complicating factors   132
Topping and tailing   133
Crossing over   134
Catching up   135

12 Strengthening visual storytelling   137

Doing, not being   138
Walk the talk   139
Swap shop   140
Valued objects   141
Say what you see   142
Trading spaces   143
Imprisoned   144
I spy   144

Compare and contrast   145
Visual pleasure   146
Sound and vision   147
Seen and not heard   148
Show, don't tell   149

13 Improving dialogue   151

Through their eyes   152
Guess who   153
Speaking relations   154
Silent talk   155
Lying and denying   156
Writing subtext   157
Key phrase   158
Exposition – creating a need to know   158
Exposition – breaking it up   159
Talking in tongues   160
The voice of the world   161

14 Managing rewrites   163

Reigniting the spark   164
Give yourself a break   164
Filtering feedback   165
Temptations   166
Building blocks   167
Running out of fuel   168
What's really going on?   169
Rhythm and tempo   170
Collapsible cast   171
Stuck in the mud   172

15 Perfecting the pitch   174

Practice runs   175
The heart of the matter   176
Finding your focus   177
Falling in love again   179
Pitching the right note   180
The spoken word   181
The question is . . .   182

16 Building outlines and treatments   184

Power punch   185
Mapping it out   186
Step to the beat   188
Bridge building   189
Warm up workout   190
Subsuming subplots   191
Purple prose   192
Title and genre   193
Naming the game   193

17 Discovering voice   195

A matter of style   196
Patchwork quilt   197
Treasure chest   198
Harmonising voices   199
Hand in hand   200
Hidden resources   201
The joy of writing   202
The writer's life   203

Conclusion   205
DIY script surgery   205

Writer's block   206
Uninspiring ideas   207
Sketchy characters   208
Insufficient plot   209
Unclear theme   210
Credibility gaps   211
Lacklustre prose   212
Never ending stories   213
Sick and tired   213
Final draft polish   214
Selling your stories   215

THE CREATIVE SCREENWRITER

Acknowledgements

Zara Waldeback would like to thank Sara Broos for supporting the continual exploration of creative screenwriting exercises both in the physical and virtual classroom, and all the students who have tried them out and revealed how they could be improved. She also wants to thank Jonathan for being a true partner and being there to listen, laugh and love the stories so they could grow and find their way; to thank Åsbacka for providing the creative space in which the book came to be heard, and to AT for always being there with magic, guidance and inspiration.

Craig Batty would like to thank his family and friends for their continued support throughout his life and career, especially when he was 'off the radar' for a while doing yet another book! He would also like to thank all of the students he has taught over the years for taking part in creative exercises and allowing them to develop. From Southampton to Portsmouth to Bournemouth to Melbourne, these students have been integral in testing out what works and what doesn't.

Both authors would like to thank our editor Jenny Ridout at Bloomsbury for being such a joy to work with and for accepting our project so wholeheartedly; Ross Fulton for taking such expert care of the letters on the page; and all at Blake Friedmann for being on our side.

Introduction

This book is both experimental and experiential. It's experimental in that no other screenwriting book focuses purely on creative exercises as a way of learning the craft. It's experiential in that the whole purpose of the book is to learn by doing; for you, the reader, to actively take part in the book and make of it what you need. You can read a lot about screenwriting, but we believe that you can learn as much, if not more, by working through a range of writing exercises that ask you to be creative and probe your work in different ways. By strategically working from the inside out, our hope is that you'll come to an understanding of screenwriting that works for you, whether in the area of character, structure, visual storytelling, dialogue, genre, voice or pitching.

By engaging in your own creative practice, you'll come to understand the techniques of screenwriting in a way that feels exciting, innovative and inherently right for you. We're not presenting a one-size-fits-all account of how to write; rather, we're outlining useful plans and dangerous pitfalls, and suggesting how to deal with them effectively. So most of the exercises in this book can be applied to different types of script projects: short and feature films, TV series and serials, experimental fusion, etc. The exercises are also intended to improve general creativity, imagination, confidence and skill, and encourage you to develop a regular creative writing workout to keep you in shape.

How to use this book

There are a few different ways to approach this book. One is simply to do the exercises in order to learn more about screenwriting. By working your way through each chapter you'll build craft skills and develop a stronger understanding of how to write scripts. If you take this approach, it's a good idea to keep a creative journal throughout the process, noting down what you learn as you work through the exercises. Having accompanying thoughts about what you experience and discover is incredibly useful for referring back to later on, and will encourage you to develop as a writer.

Another way of using the book is to improve scripts you're already working on, either professionally or for your own pleasure. Most of the exercises are applicable to your own projects, although trying them first as isolated, free-standing activities will help you better to understand the methods without worrying about specific results. Then, by applying what you learn in an exercise to a script you're developing, you should find that your scripts get better and you become more connected to and involved with them.

A third way of using this book is to dip into it as you need. If you're a professional or experienced writer, you might crave extra inspiration while working on a project. Perhaps you're stuck, or a particular part of the script isn't quite working. Or you may be aware that as a writer you have a weakness that could be refined or investigated further. The structure of the book is designed so you can delve deeper into key areas, and work with them over a dedicated period of time. The 'DIY Script Surgery' at the end of the book provides further strategies for working through frequent and familiar screenwriting problems.

DIY script surgery

It's not always possible for writers to work with script editors or experienced professionals to receive constructive feedback; but without this it can be difficult to spot problem areas in a script. The process of screenwriting has its own innate challenges, however talented or experienced you are, which is why we finish the book with 'DIY Script Surgery' – a way of addressing particular issues screenwriters often face and have to deal with. Common problems such as writer's block, selling stories and polishing final drafts are diagnosed, with a series of exercises suggested as an effective remedy. This is yet another way of using the book, and will ensure that it can continue to help and support your creative development as a screenwriter for many years to come. In fact, the idea with most of the work in this book is not only to do it once, but to keep practising and learning more about creativity, craft and your own personal voice.

Who this book is for

Actually, this book is for everyone, from beginner to professional. It offers a great way of learning screenwriting by trying things out. If you're new to it, the exercises quickly and effectively help you get to grips with the basics; if you're an experienced screenwriter, you'll find many gems to help you re-energise a project, gain new insights into your practice, and improve areas that need sharpening.

You might feel you don't need to do creative exercises; that good writers have innate talent, are born with great minds, sensitivity, awareness and creative flow; that good writers simply write, and masterpieces are born. Although this can occasionally be true, for most people being a good writer is about practice, just as it is for musicians, painters and athletes. It's about making your writing magnificent, not mediocre. That should be the aim, and we hope this book will help you achieve it.

Overall, the creative exercises in this book fulfil three essential principles:

1 The more you train and improve your craft, the more confident you'll become with your skills, and the better you'll be able to deal with problems when the going gets tough.

2 The more you turn on the tap of creativity, the more it flows. Stories become boring when they're obvious or over-familiar. By becoming more aware of how to listen out for stories, you can go beyond what you already know. Maintaining a daily creative workout develops not only technique but your ability to identify a good idea and how to fulfil its potential.

3 Using free-standing exercises can help you deal with difficulties when developing scripts under pressure. Taking time out from going round in circles with your story problems and dipping into an exercise can work wonders. Suddenly you find an idea, see how to solve a dilemma in the script, or feel re-inspired and want to get your teeth back into the screenplay.

Good writers need to understand their own writing; they need to understand the stories they're attracted to, and how best to express them. They need to be experts in the craft, confident that their practice can turn problems into assets, striking gold at every opportunity. Every writer has a unique voice waiting to be heard, and by carefully working through this book maybe you'll start to hear your voice more clearly and discover the stories longing to be told.

1 Being creative

Whatever the amount of talent you're born with, you can still train your creative muscles to improve both writing and imagination. Regular creative practice helps to 'turn on the tap' so that more ideas flow. In times of artistic drought, having a relationship with creativity helps to get the imagination moving and builds confidence by ensuring that you have the ability to do something about it.

But what does being creative mean, and how can you work with it? Creativity is about playing and about freedom: allowing you to do things for the fun of it without having to achieve set results. That said, creativity is also about restrictions. If you're completely free to do whatever you want, it can actually be difficult to generate ideas. Narrowing your options can help to kick-start creativity. When you're allowed to do whatever you want, you often follow a well-worn and familiar route; when limited, you're forced to try new ways and find different solutions you might not otherwise have thought of. So, both freedom and restriction are important in creative work.

The exercises in this chapter are about doing things for their own sake. They're not geared towards specific results, apart from helping you to become more creative and enjoy the process with confidence and ease. There are exercises you can do routinely as part of a general workout 'programme', to keep creativity flowing well and enjoy writing without the pressure of achieving. Sometimes the best ideas come when writers engage in free-standing exercises, with room to experiment and play, including doing things badly. This helps writers to change their habitual behaviour and break new ground with passion and joy.

You can do these exercises as a warm-up before the day's writing begins. This is especially useful if you're feeling stuck or uninspired. You can also do them in a group and discuss the outcomes to build more appreciation of individual writing voices and a better understanding of personal creative processes. You may also find it extremely useful to do one exercise repeatedly over a period of time.

This work will sharpen technique and strengthen certain screenwriting skills. It will also make you more aware of the world and help you interact with it as a writer should: being attentive and curious; for ever looking, listening and feeling.

What does creativity mean to you?

A good place to begin is to find out what creativity means to you, and how you might sustain a level of creativity throughout your professional life.

➢ Define your own sense of what creativity means by using the word CREATIVE to build a personal perspective on the subject. For example, being creative for one writer might mean:

  o Concentrating on what's going on around you and feeling inspired by it.

  o Reacting emotionally to life's situations.

  o Eavesdropping.

  o Actively shaping experiences into story forms.

  o Telling jokes to people in order to test out dialogue skills.

  o Investigating humanity through screen characters.

  o Valuing others' opinions of the world.

  o Exciting people by telling compelling stories.

➢ When you've built your personal definition of CREATIVE, keep it to hand, perhaps displaying it on a wall, and refer back to it every now and then to see if you're actually doing what you say. You might like to revise it over time.

Ready, steady, go!

Working with creativity on a regular basis helps to train both imagination and storytelling instincts. To be a good writer, tell as many stories, as often as you can. Writing is not only about finishing fully-fledged scripts, but experimenting with storylines all the time, even if nothing more happens to them. This exercise helps you to create a multitude of tales to see what happens when you allow yourself to write freely. Having a place to start often helps make something happen.

➢ Use one of the sentences below as the opening to a story. Set a timer for ten minutes and start writing. Don't think, just write. When the timer goes, end your story as quickly as you can, complete with resolution. This will help you practise pulling story strands together and to think about different types of endings.

   ○ *When Patrick saw what I had done, all hell broke loose.*

   ○ *I couldn't believe I lost the bag of money.*

   ○ *How much was he going to take, Gilny wondered as she waited . . .*

   ○ *I added it up again. Yes, it definitely came to five. Two and two was no longer four.*

   ○ *The horse was lame and bleeding all along the right side.*

➢ It's useful to do this once a week to keep your ideas free-flowing and get a feel for story forms. You can make up your own opening sentences, or swap with a friend or colleague. It's interesting to take the same opening sentence once a week and see what story comes out that day. Let your imagination surprise you . . .

Limiting yourself

Sometimes being faced with a limitation means you have to work harder and be more creative in the way you approach a task. This exercise will help you try new avenues by putting obstacles in your way. Working in this way isn't so much about achieving good material as about daring to try.

○ Write 500 words about your day. Write it again but this time without ever using the letter 'a'. Allow yourself to find new ways to communicate.

○ Write a description of the room you are in. Describe it again, but without using any adjectives. Instead create your impressions through unusual word combinations, sounds, rhythm and images.

○ Pick a character from one of your stories. Write them a letter of exactly 200 words, telling them what you think of them today. Write it again but say it all through subtext. Hint and suggest, maybe find a metaphor – get the message across without stating it upfront.

➢ Doing this regularly will help you become more skilled and inventive with words. Though it may seem unrelated to producing successful scripts, such everyday practice really makes a difference and helps to keep your brain active and well-oiled.

Magic moments

To be a good writer, you need to have something to write about. Our personal experiences can be interesting, but that's only a small part of life. This exercise helps you open your eyes to what is around you and find inspiration from a larger canvas. By engaging with the world writers gain awareness and understanding, and get a feeling for the moments in life that matter to them. This will feed into writing, giving actual ideas for scenes, or sharpening story instincts. It allows the element of surprise and wonder, which is particularly good when your own creative well runs dry.

➢ Think about a moment from the last week that either happened to you or that you witnessed. It should be something that sticks in your mind for some reason – maybe it moved you, puzzled, angered, scared you, or made you laugh?

➢ Describe the moment and what happened by writing it down in a few hundred words.

➢ Read it aloud and listen to what you've written. Consider how it makes you feel. Write down any responses or ideas triggered by re-experiencing the moment. Ask yourself:

- What made this moment memorable?
- What is surprising about it?
- What can you learn about the people in it?
- What made the retelling interesting? What was the most memorable detail?
- Does it make you think of any stories you want to tell?
- Why did you choose it? What did you learn about your own voice or taste from picking this moment and how you felt about it?

➤ If you do this exercise regularly (once a week is good) you'll create a whole collection of magic moments based on life rather than second-hand movies. These can help you find ideas or enrich current stories with detail, colour, life and emotion. This improves both creativity and scene writing, as it makes moments specific, surprising and authentic.

Wordplay

Being spontaneous and being forced to write something is a great way to train your brain to be creative. In this way, you're forcing yourself to think 'on the spot' and make something out of nothing. It's not about finding stories, but about playing with words and having fun.

➤ Take any word and write a story inspired by it. Just write; don't think too much about it. Spend about ten minutes on this.

➤ Now take the last letter of that word and find another word that begins with this letter, and write a story about that.

➤ Now take the last letter of that word and find another word that begins with this letter . . . and so on. For example:

- **DOG** becomes
- **GOAT** which becomes
- **TEARS** which becomes
- **SORRY** which becomes
- **YOGHURT** which becomes
- **TROUBLE** . . .

➢ Keep doing this until you have at least seven stories. Look back over them with a critical eye: do they become more creative and interesting as more stories are written? In what ways can you see this? Do you think your mind is more creative when it's had a chance to play for a while?

ABC stories

Sometimes, painting yourself into a corner and making it hard for yourself forces you to push the boundaries of what's possible. Screenwriting isn't only about ideas and structure but also about vivid sentence construction on the page. This exercise will help you unearth unusual word combinations and develop syntactic flow.

➢ Write a story where the first word begins with A, the second with B, the third with C etc., until you reach the end of the alphabet. The idea isn't to try and make it brilliant, but to create enough sense so that it has meaning. Just begin and see what happens. Don't give up if it gets too difficult. Here's an example:

  ○ *Anna bought clay ducks. Even for ghastly homes, it jarred. Kropotkin lazily meandered nearby, opening presents. Quite ravishing, she thought. Unusually vivid wonderful xtacy – yes, zizzling . . .*

Spontaneous storytelling

Telling stories verbally is excellent practice for screenwriters. It improves pitching techniques and builds rhythm, feeling and courage. With spontaneous storytelling, you make stories up on the spot and speak them out loud. This may seem difficult or nerve-wracking, but by allowing the story to form through your mouth instead of your hand, it will flow and form in a different way and exercise new creative muscles. Doing this regularly will help you hone story intution and loosen the tongue.

➢ Ask a friend, colleague or child for three things they would like in a story. It can be anything: 'dragon, ice, Wednesdays' or 'feeling blue, rollerskating, love' or 'sun, telephone, explosion', etc.

➢ Spontaneously tell a story containing all three elements, in any order. Don't plan it – throw yourself into the unknown and trust that it'll take shape as you go along. All three words need to be used at some point. Don't think too much. Keep the three words in mind and allow the story to find itself, then come to a good end. Be open – don't plan but move with the story as it comes, paying attention and following its turns and signals.

You could choose the three words yourself, but asking someone else means you throw yourself open to the winds of chance. You also have someone to tell the story to, which is important. Telling stories out loud to someone else helps you to trust both yourself and your storytelling instincts.

Listening to an onion

Listening is an essential skill for writers: listening to the world around us, moments, conversations, what's being said, what's not being said, what's really being said. We hear in many ways and it's useful for writers to focus on 'active listening'. With this, you're aware that you're listening, rather than letting it wash over you. The more you practise, the better you'll become at hearing things that may have been hidden. This exercise may seem a little strange, but can produce surprising results that show how much there is to notice in the world if only we pay attention.

➢ Find a physical object – it could be anything. Try one of these:

- ○ An onion
- ○ A tree (go outside and do this)
- ○ A blank piece of paper
- ○ Your shoes
- ○ The pillow you sleep on at night

➢ Find a quiet place and put the object in front of you. Make sure you have paper and pen. Relax and take some deep breaths. Focus on the object in front of you and say 'hello' to it. Sit calmly, and:

- ○ Write ten great things about this object
- ○ Write ten terrible things about this object
- ○ Write five highly unusual ways to use this object

> ➤ Now ask the object for a story it has to tell you, and listen to what it says. You can even say aloud 'What would you like to tell me?' or 'Please tell me a story'. This may sound silly, but works if you let it.

> ➤ Sit still and listen to the object. Begin to write whatever comes into your head. Don't censor anything, just write for as long as feels right. It can also be good to set a timer for ten to fifteen minutes. When you've finished, read the story out loud.

This kind of activity opens doors to a deeper connection with yourself and the world around you. It helps you to stop controlling every word, and increases listening skills. Whether the onion is really speaking or not is not the issue, and where the story comes from is not important. What is of interest is that it comes, and you hear it. In this way, you open up your ability to pay attention, allow stories to flow through you and accept new ideas.

Having fun!

Being creative is about having fun. It's about allowing your imagination to roam free, expressing yourself and having the confidence to put your ideas down. There's a 'science' to screenwriting, of course, such as carefully shaping narrative structure, but there's also an art to it – and art should be fun!

> ➤ Look out of the nearest window and make a note of the first thing you see: it could be an object, a person, anything. If you're already outside, then look in through a window and make a note of the first thing you see. Now look back at where you are inside (or outside), and make a note of the first thing you see there. Again, it can be anything – just choose the first thing you see.

> ➤ Put the two things together and write a story about them. You can give objects personalities if you like, or find interesting ways of matching the two things together. Write for about five minutes.

> ➤ Then look back out (or in) through the window and make a note of something else that you see. As before, go back to where you are and make a note of something else that you see. Add these two new things to the same story, and continue writing for about five minutes.

➢ Repeat this until you have a total of ten things that you're writing about in the same story. Read the story back and see if there's anything that actually works, or has the potential to work. Do any of the combinations create an interesting approach to a story idea? Is there something that makes the juxtaposed elements spark off another idea? Are you inspired actually to take something forward from this into a project?

Being bad

The pressure of writing can sometimes stifle creative juices. Nothing emerges apart from vast empty silence. If you feel like this, or as if whatever you write is turgid, trite and terrible, try this exercise. Here you can be as bad as you like. In fact, the badder the better . . .

➢ Write a short dialogue scene based on the following:

Carla wants a new pair of shoes. Stephan wants to give her whatever she desires but knows they're already dangerously in debt.

o First, try to write the scene and dialogue as badly as you possibly can. Make the characters over the top and stereotyped, choose stupid words, hackneyed sentences, forget any sense of rhythm. Allow yourself the treat of being truly awful.

o Read through what you've written and rewrite it – but this time make it even worse! Maybe it's not possible, but try. Go totally over the top or bore yourself silly.

o Finally, put it aside and write the scene again. Write it the way you want to write it. Forget about being bad or good and simply allow the characters to say what they want to say and what you want to hear them talk about. Read through and see what surprises you. What new information or feelings came through this?

Writing in a 'bad' way can be very helpful occasionally, since it tends to get you out of deadlock, and releases debilitating thoughts about what you mustn't say. If you're writing a scene and feel it's not working, allow yourself to do it badly first. If nothing else, you'll have had some fun and relaxed, and stopped trying so hard – all of which normally helps you get back on track to writing well.

2 Generating ideas

One of the main things that will sell a script is the quality of its idea. Day after day, those working in development are inundated by scripts that are well written yet lack something. A good writer is not only someone who can write well; a good writer has something to say and expresses it in a way that touches people, moving them and getting them to think about the world. One part of becoming a successful screenwriter is to practise writing craft; another is to train yourself to detect and develop good ideas.

People sometimes assume that the mainstream film and TV industry is not interested in unusual ideas; that they only seek to re-make old, familiar stories. This is true to some extent, and there are genres and audience conventions to consider, but exciting, engaging and powerful ideas always have a good chance. Many screenwriters pick weak ideas that are over-familiar or unsuitable for the screen. Developing skills that help you find not just good but great ideas can make a huge difference to your career. It's not just how you write but what you write that will define what kind of writer you are.

The exercises in this chapter will guide you through ways of sourcing ideas and testing whether they're worth further development. They'll encourage you to work with a range of screenwriting techniques that will deepen your understanding and your ability to detect story ideas in everyday encounters. Overall, the exercises will equip you with story-finding skills that will be valuable across your whole writing career.

Going to the heart

There's no getting away from the fact that if you want to be a screen-writer, you have to have something to say. Whether it's funny or serious, you're engaging in an act of communication. So, when think-ing about what story to tell, think about what's in your heart. What do you really care about? What are you yearning and burning to tell the world about? What's itching under your skin?

➢ It's important that writers collect thoughts, ideas and feelings to develop a personal writing territory. There are many ways of doing this, but here are some that can help. Choose at least one of the following and commit to doing it regularly:

  ○ Keep a daily journal where you write about things that are inter-esting, difficult, memorable or moving.

  ○ Cut out stories or pictures from newspapers and magazines that catch your interest, and keep them in a scrapbook.

  ○ Build a list of interesting quotations that spark your imagination.

  ○ Find 'Magic moments' once a week (see Chapter 1).

  ○ Keep a notebook in which you write down ideas that come to you – even if it's just a scene, word, theme or character. Sometimes it takes years for an idea to sprout, so keep it safe to make sure it doesn't get lost and forgotten.

➢ Choose one way of collecting interesting personal material. Begin to do it today. You can work with it in different ways. For instance, every week look at it and randomly choose one image, quotation or idea and brainstorm twenty different story possibilities. Or, choose two or three items from your collection and put them together to see what happens.

Such collections are great tools for writers. You can dip into them when you need inspiration and you always have material to get your mind and heart moving.

Finding the plot, finding the emotion

Good screenwriting isn't just about creating a plot that works well, but creating an emotional throughline for that plot. An audience should be taken on an emotional journey through the experience of the protagonist or protagonists. As such, it's as important to find the emotion of a story as it is to find its plot or narrative shape. Often, an idea for a plot is exciting, maybe even highly original, but it's the job of the screenwriter to find the universal quality in that plot – the emotion that stops it from being a series of hollow and meaningless actions.

> Look through a selection of newspapers and find at least five stories. Go for smaller, more isolated stories rather than bigger, international stories that might have been developing for days or longer. Sketch out the basic plot of the five stories: what happens, to whom, where, how and why? If you find it helpful, write out the plot according to a basic model of narrative structure that you know.

> Now brainstorm at least five emotional qualities or values associated with each story. Ask yourself what the story really is or could be about, and what the emotions of those involved are or might be. You should look for potential themes and universal qualities, focusing on the characters of the story and how their situation might be felt by others if dramatised.

> Using these emotional qualities, map a range of possible character journeys (emotional arcs) across each story, and decide which might have the most appeal: a) for an audience to experience; and b) for you to write. You'll probably need to think beyond the mere story given, using it as one moment or sequence within a broader narrative.

Into the unknown

Ideas come not only from things you know you're interested in, but from places you didn't even know existed. Allowing yourself to wander into uncharted territory and seeing what you find can be exciting and fruitful. This is great if you feel all your ideas sound the same and you're tired of them. It's a good way of turning off conscious control and diving under the surface. With this exercise, do it stage by stage and don't look ahead.

1   Take one word and brainstorm a list of fifteen other words that relate to it. It can be any word; pick one out of a dictionary or use one of the following: **green – rain – yesterday – lotus – feet.**

2 Look at your fifteen words and choose one word from them – it can be one that interests you, irritates, bores or amuses you.

3 Write your new word at the top of a piece of paper. Write a list of ten other words you think of in relation to this word.

4 From this list of ten new words, pick three, either at random or ones that appeal to you in some way, even if you don't know why.

5 Use these three words to create a story. Write 500 words and give the story a beginning, middle and end. Read it and see how it feels. What interests you that you can develop further? If not the story, maybe a situation, feeling or character?

This deceptively simple exercise can activate surprising and powerful stories. The trick is to have a short time to do it in, and go through a gradual process away from thinking into intuition and feeling. This opens up ideas that may otherwise not be heard. If nothing much happens, keep practising, using a different first word each time.

➤ Try writing your own list of fifty words to explore, words you like the sound of, ones that appall you, that you overuse, are afraid of, love or feel mystified by. Whenever you feel like finding a secret story, pick a word and see what it has in store.

What's around you?

Ideas are all around us. Wherever we turn, whether in our own environment or an unfamiliar one, there's something that can be turned into an idea. Identifying story potential will be dealt with in Chapter 3, but for now the intention is to help you gather ideas.

➤ Go to a place where you know you'll find things that either you haven't seen or used for a while, or things you don't know at all. It could be a drawer or a cupboard or a closed box, for example. Look in this place and take out (if possible) a few objects. One by one, make notes about the objects, notes that might lead you to finding narrative triggers. These triggers might be factual or fictional, but should be ideas or values that could have story potential. The following questions might help you:

○ How old is the object?

○ Who used it last?

○ Where was it made?

○ Who owns it?

○ Who would like to own it?

○ What significance does it hold?

○ What memory does it bring up for you?

○ What do you want to do with it now?

○ Where would you like to move it to?

➢ Once you've made notes on each object, review them. What stands out to you about them? How might you develop them into story ideas? Now put the objects together and see if there's a story to tell that incorporates everything.

Creative collisions

Creativity is not always about originality and inventing something from scratch. Sometimes writers become obsessed with finding brand new never-before-seen material that will stun the world. Creativity is also about putting existing things together in unexpected, unusual ways. By combining elements, you create new situations, relationships and possibilities, where magic occurs without being forced.

➢ There are many ways of doing this. Try these:

1   Write something you like, then something you hate. Add five reasons why you like it, five why you hate it. Now write five reasons why someone might like what you hate, and why someone might hate what you like. Who would these people be? What stories could they tell?

2   Choose an object from your childhood. Choose another from your life right now. Put them together with a third object that doesn't exist, but which you've just invented. What kind of situations could arise? Who would use them, and how?

3   Think of a place you've never been, and one you know only too well. Create two characters, one for each place, then make them

swap places. What kind of stories could come from each character-place combination? If there's one character who could live in both worlds, who would that be?

Connections between elements can be made in many ways: emotional, linguistic, narrative, practical. Think laterally. Create lists around each element if you'd like to go deeper before exploring actual ideas. Play around with ideas and different ways of putting them together until you find a combination that feels right. Who knows what's waiting in the wings . . . ?

Bringing people together

Many ideas arise out of an interest in people, whether they're real or characters in a story. Characters can provide a treasure trove of stories if only you have a key to unlock them. By combining characters, you create natural action and reaction, conflict, challenges and situations. Stories built organically from characters are often rich, solid and engaging as they tend to arise naturally from the situation.

➢ Pick two characters you already have, but from different stories. Put them together and see what happens. How do they react to each other? What happens between them? How do they push each other's buttons? What conflicts ensue? What objectives do they share? Where could they meet?

➢ Think about what attracts them to each other and what repels them, what brings them together (connections) and what pushes them apart (conflicts). Do this with many different character combinations, until you find an idea you want to develop into a story.

➢ Once you've discovered an interesting relationship, introduce a third character into the mix. Often character triangles create the strongest drama (not just love triangles but with all kinds of tensions and dynamics), so see what happens.

The eventual idea that comes from putting the characters together may not involve them. What comes out of their combination may lead you somewhere else altogether. Don't stay married to the idea of keeping the original characters, if you feel more interesting material reveals itself along the way.

What do you know? What don't you know?

When trying to find ideas, it's sometimes good to put aside the obvious things that you know in favour of finding out things you don't know. This makes you think harder and more creatively, and can avoid bland, clichéd ideas emerging. For example, you might know that your friend has a twin brother, but you probably don't know what they did the last time they met up. Where did they go? What did they say? What were their feelings towards each other? Crucially, how does all of this relate to them being twins? By dreaming up ideas about what they did when they last met up you're training your creative mind to make interesting connections between the known and the unknown. You're actively trying to find story ideas by 'flipping' knowledge into lack of knowledge in the hope that something interesting might emerge.

➢ Take the following scenario:

> *Daniel is an eleven-year-old boy who has just opened the ultimate*
> *Christmas present: a sporty, dazzling, red bike. He's absolutely*
> *elated. It's the best Christmas present he's ever had. It's what he's*
> *been dreaming of.*

○ Think of as many things as you can that you don't know about the scenario, things that might connect with what is known. Don't settle for the first idea that comes into your head; keep pushing so that you have an extensive and wide-ranging list.

○ How many ideas did you come up with? What range of ideas? Was there a common theme? Did your ideas relate specifically to the scenario set, such as a young boy at Christmas? How much do you know about the world given? How much did you veer away from the specifics of the world? Were your ideas mainly concerned with character or plot? Did any of your ideas have potential to work in a variety of genres and forms?

➢ Now try the exercise again but with something that you've witnessed from real life. Again, try to push your questions in interesting and different ways so that they will stretch beyond the obvious. Use the following as a skeleton framework:

> *Think about a person who you saw on a journey today or yesterday,*
> *maybe someone you saw while walking down the street or on a bus*

or train. List five things you know about that person from what you saw. Now list five things you don't know about that person, linking them where possible to the known facts. You might also link these unknown facts to the journey they were undertaking when you saw them: where were they going, and why?

Words of wisdom

Sometimes, what people say can affect and inspire you even more than what they do. A line of dialogue or a catchphrase, whether addressed to you or overheard, can ignite meaning within you and spark ideas for story possibilities. Such words can give you a great opening for a screenplay, a wonderful ending, a recurring phrase that carries thematic meaning, or even a specific line that you can use at a key narrative turning point.

➢ Take the following lines of dialogue and brainstorm ideas about how they could be used in a story. Think structurally (where might the line be placed?), thematically (what might the line mean?) and pragmatically (who might be saying this, and for what reason?). When you have a story idea for each, summarise it in no more than 300 words.

    ○ *You tried and you failed. I tried and I succeeded. I think that's all you need to know, buddy.*

    ○ *Just give it a push. No, not like that. Use both hands. Here, try the gloves.*

    ○ *How can I trust you when I don't even know who you are?*

➢ Now listen out for your own words of wisdom, keeping a dramatic ear open in your everyday life. If you hear something that resonates in any way at all, make a note of it. Each time, create at least five story ideas.

Trading places

One problem with ideas is that they can feel too familiar. It's important to explore an idea fully at an early stage before doing too much writing. Often, writers stop at the first step without thinking about how to develop ideas further into something more fresh and interesting. One way of seeing what else an idea might contain is to work with opposites, trying something completely different. It can feel like too big a change, but it pays off to be bold. Sometimes it creates a new idea and sometimes it simply helps to loosen things up.

➤ Try the following to shake up ideas with opposites:

○ Transform your protagonists. Give them opposite characteristics to what they have, trying them one at a time. If they're female, make them male, and vice versa. If they're old, make them young. Give them the opposite goal/want/dream to what they have now. Put them in the opposite situation to where they were in the beginning.

○ Switch protagonist and antagonist. What happens if you make your current antagonist into your protagonist? What happens to plot and theme? What if the protagonist was really the antagonist – who would be your protagonist then?

○ Change worlds. If your story takes place in a normal, everyday world, try setting it in a fantastical place or different time period.

○ Trade genres. If you're writing a thriller, try it as a comedy. If you think it's a drama, try it as a western, sci-fi or children's story. If you think it's a romance, make it into a horror. Not all stories fit all genres, and you may not want to change for good, but by trading places in this way you open up interesting new ideas.

○ Swap endings. If you have a happy ending, make it sad. If you have a sad ending, make it happy. What happens to the story? How would the structure have to change?

In the news

Newspapers and magazines are a rich source of inspiration for developing stories. By their very nature they bring together a whole host of situations, characters and emotions, and shape them into bite-sized stories for mass consumption. For the screenwriter, looking at what's in the news can be inspiring since it offers a range of narrative triggers that can be explored further. Reported stories and interviews, and even headlines, can provide a lot of fuel for ideas. In this way, creativity comes from using existing material and taking it much further than currently presented.

➢ Take a newspaper or magazine and cut out a selection of headlines. Some may be long; some may be short. See if you can create a logical story by laying them all out in some kind of order. Of course it won't make total sense, but see how far you can get. It's worth considering the range of headline styles: some are very factual, whereas some are quite emotive and aim for the shock factor.

➢ For this exercise, you may find that particular headlines lend themselves to particular story moments, such as turning points, plot twists and dramatic revelations. See how many different stories you can get out of the same headlines by putting them in different orders, and how many you can make in different styles or genres.

The hardest choice

Some writers have no problem coming up with ideas or finding things they want to write about. But having many ideas brings a new difficulty: choice. And no one but the writer can decide which idea to develop. Others can offer advice, expertise and experience, and if a producer employs you they can certainly instruct you in what to write, but in other situations it's the writer who has to make the choice.

Selecting and standing by your idea is part of the writer's commitment to the story. It's important to know you've chosen well, and taken the time to decide. It's not always obvious, and even if it is, this exercise is a good one for discovering whether the one idea you have is potent enough – or if you need to go back to the drawing board.

➢ Answer these questions for each idea you're considering:

  ○ How do I feel when I think of exploring this idea?

  ○ How do I feel when I think of spending time with these characters?

  ○ How do I feel when I think of spending a lot of time with these characters?

  ○ How do I feel when I think of spending time in this world?

O How do I feel when I think of never writing anything else than this?

O What do I want from this project? Is it a writing sample, or is it for production? What's important for me to achieve at this point in my career, and which script will best do this for me?

O What are the opportunities and challenges in this idea in relation to the industry?

O What's the 'USP' (Unique Selling Point) of this idea?

O Why does this idea 'fit' me? Why do we 'fit' each other?

O What skills/techniques/writing craft will it help me to improve?

O What most excites me about this idea?

O What most scares me?

O What most bores me?

O What is the risk in choosing it?

O Why am I the right person to tell this story?

➤ Finally, ask yourself:

O How would I feel if I never told this story?

O How would I feel if I didn't tell this story now?

➤ Weigh up the answers both in a practical, realistic way and by listening to your gut feeling. One aspect can outweigh all others if it feels important enough – it may not make sense, but feels right. In the end, the choice is yours, and it's good to know you've made it well.

Perfect fit

Some ideas need a particular form to work. Others are possible to adapt between forms. Part of finding a good idea is knowing how best to express it. It's important to respect this and take time to discover the perfect fit for an idea. Once you're sure you have a good idea you want to develop, the question is whether it will work for the screen (TV or film), or would be better as a novel, theatre or radio play.

➤ To test an idea's suitability for the screen, ask:

O Does the character have a clear objective?

O Is there a series of obstacles to the character's objective?

- How easy is it to find ways to externalise the character's emotions?
- Can the character's objective be played out through action?
- Does the story fit into a genre, or does it mix genres in an interesting way?

A film or TV idea may not answer all these questions neatly, but if there's an issue with every single question you may need to find an idea that is better suited for the screen.

Once you've decided that your idea is right for the screen, consider whether it's best told as a short, feature film or TV series. What would benefit the story you want to tell? Stay away from personal prejudices and shoehorning ideas into a format because you think it's what you want to write. It's the story which needs to tell you.

➤ Take this basic premise:

   Zoe travels to an unknown territory to find a lost cargo ship.

- Write a one-page outline of this idea as a short film.
- Write a one-page outline of it as a feature film.
- Write a one-page outline of it as a TV series.

➤ How does it change? What has to be added and subtracted? Does it work for all formats, or is one best? What does each format need? How can you tell it'll work in a particular format?

➤ Now try the same exercise with one of your own ideas, keeping an open mind and feeling your way towards the right format.

3

Developing stories

Once an idea is decided upon, it needs to be prised open to cultivate the story within it. The idea is just the seed, and hopefully you'll have chosen a strong one with plenty of life in it, but you still need to make sure it blossoms. A good idea doesn't automatically become a good story unless it's enriched through character, world, theme and plot. So this chapter looks at how to take the germ of an idea and investigate what stories it might hold, and how to take the right steps towards building a strong narrative.

But what exactly is a 'story'? There are many ways to approach this question: a story can be plot (a sequence of events); it can be an emotional journey (a character arc); it can be an exploration of a world; a series of problems and solutions; a desire to reach a goal or realise a dream. In reality, a story is all these things. It's essentially the presentation of a chain of related events with cohesive meaning that together create something larger than the sum of their parts.

Story development often arises naturally when working with character and structure, and these areas are dealt with in other chapters of the book. This chapter looks at how to grow a story from the seed of an idea, in terms of both plot and theme. To do this it's important to understand the relationship between them, and why it's necessary to work on both levels when developing a script.

Growing up

Finding a good idea is an achievement in itself, but it doesn't mean you've found the actual story. One idea can contain many different stories. It can be told from different perspectives, emphasising different themes, in different genres or tones. The same idea can be given to different writers and they'll all find something different to say. After settling on an idea, take time to explore the many stories you may find in it. There may be some you've not yet considered.

➢ Look at the idea below and the four possible stories that come out of it. Define the differences between them in terms of theme, tone and plot.

IDEA

○ *Twenty-five-year-old Lil approaches Marion and tells her she's her long-lost niece. Marion's not had any contact with half-brother Steve for twenty years, and didn't know he had children. She invites Lil in and they develop a stumbling relationship which makes Marion question what family really means to her.*

POTENTIAL STORIES

○ *Marion finds it difficult to believe Lil. She becomes obsessed with trying to discover the truth behind who she is and why she's here. It brings back painful memories of betrayal from her childhood, and Marion rejects Lil.*

○ *Marion has a perfectly happy life and doesn't need anyone else. She feels obliged to let Lil stay as she's family, but doesn't appreciate being saddled with a young woman who needs to be taught a thing or two about life. Or is it Marion who's forgotten how to live?*

○ *Marion always regretted losing contact with Steve and is delighted Lil has turned up. She sees her as the way back and convinces Lil to help her heal the family rift, even when Lil decides it's too difficult and doesn't want to be part of it.*

○ *As Marion and Lil live together, they start to like each other. Then Marion discovers Lil has lied and isn't family at all. Lil admits she's very lonely and longs for family. The women decide they can form their own family if they want, and Lil becomes the daughter Marion never had.*

> ➢ Which story appeals to you most? What feels interesting in terms of its dramatic possibilities? What does each tell you about the theme of family?

> ➢ Now come up with three further possible storylines from this idea. Which do you like? How can you find others? Have you turned the idea inside out and looked at all its aspects? Try doing it to your own ideas and see what you find.

Finding your compass

When building a story from an idea, it can be easy to lose sight of your target. Whatever its structure, a good script needs a central focus so the story can find its way home. If you're not clear what it's really about, it's easy to get lost during rewriting, especially when a myriad new ideas may tumble into the story from exploration and feedback.

One of the best ways to keep focus is to find the *Central Dramatic Question* (CDQ). Once defined, it can work as a compass guiding the writer through the many dramatic decisions they have to make during development. It's also good to locate the *Central Thematic Question* (CTQ). This is related to the CDQ, but exists on a deeper level. The CDQ usually refers to events and actions in the plot, whereas the CTQ expresses the character's need and writer's intent.

Because it's a question, the CDQ creates active need and drama. This central question runs through the whole story as it develops and is the beating heart of the plot. The thematic question is asked in all the main characters' storylines and looked at from different angles. It guides the depth of the character arcs, relationships, structure and tone. For instance:

CDQ: *Will they save the museum from commercial developers?*
CTQ: *Will they learn to see the true treasures it houses?*

CDQ: *Will he escape from the violent mafia gang?*
CTQ: *Will he leave his old life behind and find a new way of being?*

CDQ: *Will she solve the mystery behind the court case?*
CTQ: *Will she decide which side she's on and what her true commitment is?*

> Take three films or TV series you know well. Write the CDQ and CTQ for each in one or two short sentences. How do the two questions relate to each other? What do you learn from seeing the two together?

> Now try it on your own script. Work out the CDQ and CTQ, then go through the story and see how they guide it. Are they in every sequence, every scene? Does the story veer away from this centre and go off on tangents? What dramatic decisions do you need to take to bring it back to the essential questions? After working on the script, the CDQ and CTQ may change. Write them out again and check against your plot. They will be your guiding stars through development and help you find your way when you get lost.

Assessing story potential

Finding a story from a character's situation is a skill that should be practised by all screenwriters. Working with known facts about a character can allow a screenwriter's imagination to roam free and make interesting, creative interpretations that give potential for original stories. This can then be assessed and honed down into a workable project. In this way, the process becomes a combination of creative thinking and critical reflection; dreaming up ideas and then analysing them in context.

> Read the following summary and consider the potential within it for a screenplay. Use the information as character backstory and how a credible story might emerge from the facts given. Who is the character? Who isn't he? What drives him? What holds him back? What's his current life situation and how might he feel about it? What might the future hold, or not hold? What could his specific dreams be? What things might he want? What are his strengths and weaknesses?

> *Al Zuckerman is a twenty-nine-year-old overweight man who lives in Minneapolis, USA. He's a single child and lives with his mother; his father died when Al was just fifteen. Since the age of seventeen he has worked in the bakery section of his local supermarket. At weekends he plays for the Midwest Green Jocks, a low-performing, non-league American football team. He has a limited number of*

friends, most of whom he works with, and he often finds himself the butt of jokes and the scapegoat for failure within the football team. He was dating Carla between the ages of seventeen and nineteen, but sadly she died in a freak accident. Al hasn't been able to date, or find anyone suitable to date, since. He carries the weight of the family on his shoulders because his mother never got over his father's death. He dreams of being someone, and somewhere, else.

➢ Once you've considered Al's story potential, write short outlines for five different screenplays. Try to vary the genre, style and tone of each. Whilst doing this, ask yourself what it is about the character's life that attracts you to telling that story. What are you most interested in, and why?

What's the problem?

At the heart of an idea is often a problem: a character can't get what they want, a world is in trouble, a relationship is in conflict. One way of making sure that the story doesn't get stuck in the initial situation and just treads water is to develop the problem. Looking at what can go wrong for a character is a productive way to build story from an idea. It forces characters into reactions, actions and decisions, and makes the journey move. By locating the problem and asking how it can continually change, a story is naturally formed.

➢ Take this example:

Mickey's involved in a sales scam where he checks out home security and the gang he's in robs the right places. He doesn't care about hurting people but is angry at being bossed around by the leader. He wants to be rich and respected, and takes risks to prove his worth to the gang.

➢ How can Mickey's problem get worse? What could go wrong?

○ *Mickey's arrested by the police and forced to inform on his gang.*

○ *He's beaten up by a homeowner who's been robbed and wants revenge.*

○ *He's set up by the leader to take the blame for a break-in that went wrong.*

o *The leader spreads lies about him and humiliates him in front of the gang.*

o *He's excluded from the gang after beating up the leader.*

o *He sets up a daredevil stunt to impress the gang but injures himself badly.*

o *He realises the gang wants to rob his sister's house and refuses to do it.*

o *He loses everything after someone breaks in to his place and robs it.*

o *The leader's wife falls in love with him and wants to have an affair.*

o *Mickey falls in love with the leader.*

➢ Now find ten to fifteen ways that the problem in the following premise can get worse:

> *Alkina wants to go to the moon. She's trained for many years to be an astronaut and has just been accepted on the new UN Space programme.*

➢ What could stop her? What could thwart her ambitions and why? Look at the problems you create and see how they fit together. Do any form a natural sequence? Do they all belong in the same story, or tell different tales? Choose the best five, then write story outlines where you allow the problems to spin the plot forward.

This method enables an idea to be plotted out very quickly. You then have to decide whether it's the story you want to tell. Just because it's dramatic doesn't mean it's the best set of events. See also 'Deepening the problem' and 'Rising action' in Chapter 6 on how to work further with problems as a way of structuring a story.

Dot to dot

A good test when developing a feature project is asking this simple question: does enough happen? There should be strong, credible and progressive narrative developments that challenge and change the characters, and engage the audience. A writer may have an idea for a feature, but there's only enough material for a short; so an important part of story development is mapping out what happens and judging if it's enough.

➤ From the point-of-view of developing a feature film, use the following key plot points to map out a full narrative with at least thirty beats. The plot points are deliberately basic and sparse; the task is to find enough interesting material within the idea to move the story between the plot points. Extract as much as you can from the implied character journeys, remembering that a feature narrative should have obstacles, tests, twists, turns, and character and plot revelations. If you wish, 'beat out' the plot in bullet-point form first, then summarise it as a prose outline.

> *Miranda feels lonely and unloved → She meets a guy who intrigues her → She decides to try and woo him → She almost gives up → They get married*
>
> *Harry is down on his luck → He gets the chance to steal money and does so → He finds himself on the run from a dangerous mob → He's almost killed → He gives the money to a charity*
>
> *Hannah and Greg both lose their jobs → They decide to go on a road trip → They enjoy themselves at first → Then they start to irritate each other → They decide to go their separate ways → They meet back where they started and both reveal a secret to each other*

➤ Look back at each idea. Do you think there's enough for a feature? If not, why not? Which idea do you like best, and why? Is your preference related to the plot that you have constructed or the emotional journey that the character travels?

➤ Try the exercise again, but this time take each story in a new direction by working in a different genre. Which elements change radically, and which stay the same? Again, is there enough material for a feature?

Conflict vs meaningful conflict

Conflict is often a key word in screenwriting. It's seen as the core aspect of drama, and problems are a great way of making something happen. But conflict by itself does not make a narrative. Initially, it's simply a series of events. What makes it a story is the overarching meaning that the conflict creates. You can't build plot through problems alone; you have to know its purpose and that it's taking the character (and the audience) in the right direction.

For instance, if *Frida wants to buy a horse*, there could be a number of conflicts standing in her way, such as not having enough money, her partner not letting her do it, her not knowing anything about horses, having been banned by the Horse Association, or maybe being only five years old. How do you tell which is the right kind of obstacle?

By considering CDQ, CTQ and character arc, you should be able to find the right kind of plot problems. Each obstacle should push the character further on their journey, complicate it in an appropriate way, and offer some kind of help for the character to fulfil their need. This way each conflict comes packed with the power to transform and guide, even if it's in a roundabout way.

> If Frida's story is about battling cancer and getting well through the help of her horse, all conflicts need to relate to this in some way, and help her move through the various stages of her journey.

> Brainstorm seven possible clear conflicts that could be part of this story. How does each conflict help and hinder Frida? How does each complicate the story, and help make her better or worse? What are the different ways that she needs to get well (not only physically but emotionally or even spiritually)? What hidden gift does each conflict bring with it, by intention or by chance? How does she come into contact with a horse? How does it help her? How does her relationship to the horse change through the different potential conflicts? What would the next dramatic step be for Frida after each obstacle?

> Create an arc for Frida's journey with seven story steps, each including a meaningful conflict. Is there a clear inner and outer journey? Does it express the heart of the story and generate the right feel?

This is one of the most important pieces of work you can do to create a cohesive credible script that will engage the audience and is well worth spending time on.

What happens next?

A screenplay narrative should keep turning. It should propel the story forward in credible and interesting ways, creating intrigue, suspense and surprise. Audiences should be constantly asking themselves, 'What happens next?' Genres such as horror and action adventure lend themselves extremely well to this, with the plot continually moving forward. Even genres such as romance and coming-of-age adopt the same principle, albeit in more subtle ways. When developing a story you should think carefully about the sequence of events you're using to tell that story and whether it has enough energy and drive.

➤ For this exercise, think from an audience's point of view about what might be appealing to watch and engage with. With the given story starting points, develop fully-fledged stories by continually asking 'What happens next?' Flesh out at least three versions of each story, using a different genre each time, taking it as far as you can. Aim for at least twenty plot points for each story, thinking carefully about how each action/reaction fuels the next action/reaction.

Freddy is a forty-year-old man who lives with his mother. He's never flown the nest, never had a proper relationship, and doesn't work. He's been looking after his mother for most of his life, and although he doesn't quite know it, that's the way she likes to keep it. One day, when Freddy's collecting her tablets from the chemist, his mother falls down the stairs at home and dies.

Sandra's been having strange nightmares recently. She keeps seeing a young girl, whom she doesn't recognise, coming towards her with a bloodstained night dress and a knife in her hand. More alarmingly, the young girl keeps calling Sandra 'Mummy'. Sandra tries to block the nightmares out of her mind but nearly has a heart attack when one day she sees the young girl waiting at her front door.

Alvin's besotted by Clara, his childhood sweetheart. The problem is that Clara doesn't see Alvin in this way; to her, he's more like a brother. They're both turning eighteen, and when the summer comes to an end they'll be setting off for different universities in different parts of the country. Alvin's adamant that they'll continue to be special friends, but with a good seven hours' drive between them it's hard to see how they'll stay close. Alvin doesn't know what to do.

➤ Look back at the stories you've fleshed out and ask someone to read them and comment on their appeal. A simple yet effective question to ask your reader is: 'Did the narrative development hook and interest you?' If the answer is no, probe the story further and find ways of improving it.

One thing leads to another

A fruitful, easy way to build story is to allow cause and effect to flow into a natural sequence of events. Not only does this create plot quickly, it also acts as glue connecting the story together. By seeing how one action affects another, the audience understands how characters feel, what they want, what they should expect. A story where scenes have little sense of relationship to each other often makes the story seem lacking in purpose. By working with cause and effect, the story forms a whole where each part feeds into the next and creates ever-deepening meaning.

➤ To use cause and effect as a story-making tool, start somewhere important, then simply turn each step over so it has a knock-on effect. You don't need to think ahead, nor do you not need to know where you're going; simply stay in the moment with the action and ask what happens next. The more you know your characters, the better this works. Here's a sequence built from one step to the next:

Richard finds the schedule for the ferry boat to a nearby island.

The phone rings. It's his mother, wanting to know when he'll visit.

She keeps him on the phone for too long.

Richard's late and cycles too fast to get to the harbour.

He slips on the wet road and falls off.

A woman nearly runs him over but stops just in time.

He's furious with her, though more angry with himself (and his mum).

The woman offers to take him to the cottage she's renting.

He refuses, but she insists as he's in shock.

She takes him back and gives him tea and biscuits. They talk.

They realise they have something in common from the past – she's come to research her family history and Richard knows something secret that happened on the island forty years ago. During the summer she befriends him to find out what really happened.

➢ Read the sequence again to analyse how each step leads to the next. There should be a natural effect where each moment flows into a change, which the characters have to react to and act on. Every action causes a new reaction, every reaction a new action.

➢ Try it with a new idea. Locate five major points in the idea, starting with the beginning where something vital happens. At each of these moments, take what you have and walk forward one step at a time. Keep going for as long as you can, staying in the moment to feel what the next natural reaction would be.

Back to the future

As well as stepping forwards, it can sometimes be useful to step backwards as a way of connecting story steps. It can be particularly useful for thrillers, mysteries and romantic comedies as it helps to twist and turn the plot and create surprises. It can work wonders when you know where you need to get to in a story, but can't find a satisfactory way of reaching it.

By working backwards, you allow the brain to take a break from the normal pathways and find new solutions and possibilities. Again it requires working one step at a time, creating a reverse logic where the outcome is already fixed. At each step you ask: 'How did they get here?' and then write what happened before. By working only one step at a time you come to more original results that also feel solid and credible. Moments when the story really surprises an audience are often thrilling, so this technique is invaluable in lifting the storytelling to another level.

> *It's the end of the story, and Julio realises Christie has been lying to him. Ricky, the child he thought was her husband's, is actually his. During the story he's come to love Ricky, and as he realises he's his actual son, he accepts him with his heart. However, at the end of Act Two, Julio told Christie he wanted nothing more to do with either her or Ricky, thinking that she'd been unfaithful with a third man.*

➢ Which story steps could lead Julio from the end of Act Two, where he rejects Christie and Ricky, to accepting Ricky as his son by the end? How could these steps surprise the audience?

➤ Start with the end step of Julio accepting Ricky as his son, then work backwards asking 'How did they get here?'. Write five to seven steps that will link the two in a credible and interesting way.

In Chapter 8 you'll find the related exercise 'Full stop' which explores the idea of shaping good endings further.

Losing the plot

Good screenplays should take an audience on an emotional as well as a physical journey, giving them a strong sense of the themes and meaning underpinning the narrative. The primary way that this can be achieved is through the character journey. When an audience watches a character act and react under pressure, what they're really watching is an emotional reaction to a situation where actions are imbued with theme and meaning. In this way it's the emotional journey of the character that takes on a deeper and longer-lasting impression than the physical events they've gone through.

Sometimes, literally 'losing the plot' and concentrating on what your story's really about can help you create a screenplay with a deeper heart and a much wider appeal, touching the audience with its universal themes and meaning. Here, the plot that's needed to convey the themes and meaning will emerge in its own right, and hopefully the screenplay will take its own organic shape.

➤ Choose a film or TV drama that you're familiar with. Note down what you think it's about, thematically: what does it mean to you? Pull away from thinking of just the plot; instead, tap into the underlying meaning that speaks to you.

➤ Write a summary of what the story says to you, about its thematic intentions; you might want to call this a 'Statement of Intent'. Keep rewriting this until you've got a clear, succinct summary of about 300 words. Make it as evocative and personal as you like, as long as it clearly states how the script is affecting you.

➤ Finally, revisit the film or TV drama and work out how key plot points relate to its thematic intentions. Pick the moments that stand out to you as having thematic or meaningful value, and summarise how the plot is used to tell the emotion. Try to understand how the script has been structured dramatically to give it an impact thematically.

4 Understanding characters

Characters are the lifeblood of screenplays. In nearly all stories, it's through a character that the audience experiences plot and theme, and comes to understand what the writer wants to communicate. Characters are the purveyors of meaning and, if executed well, can smuggle all sorts of symbolism and subtext into their emotional baggage.

A well-designed character has within it a natural movement towards story. By engaging in physical action and experiencing emotional reactions, a character will generate plot through their desire to achieve or reach a goal. And, because this plot has been generated by the character, more resonance is brought to the story. Knowing your characters inside out is thus an essential requirement for all writing, and a perfect starting point for investigating the potential of your script.

A character isn't just a handy device to hang the plot on, but a real, live person – in the story, at least. They need to be treated as such, and made believable. They don't have to be sympathetic, but should be empathetic. They may start out as a basic archetype, but with further exploratory work can be transformed into a complex character that supports the deep structure of the story and invites the audience into its heart.

Working with character is a useful strategy during any point of development, writing or redrafting, and will often bring new ideas to the table. As such, the exercises in this chapter will help you to understand your characters more and give you an enriched sense of what's really going on in your story.

Pinpointing the protagonist

The protagonist is the main character of a story, the person who the audience will connect with most strongly and through whose eyes they will see the story. It's important to choose the protagonist wisely; you may feel it's obvious who it is, but it's good to reflect on why and whether there are other possibilities. It's also useful to clarify what it is in a protagonist and their journey that you as writer feel attracted to.

Strong protagonists often have some of these attributes:

- Has the biggest problem.
- Has the furthest to go (the longest arc).
- Undergoes the biggest change.
- Engages the audience (empathy vs sympathy).
- Provides connection between audience and story.
- Takes action (though not always).

➤ Considering your own story, ask yourself:

- What's it really about?
- What's its theme?
- Where does it start and where does it end emotionally?
- Why do I want to tell it?

➤ Map your answers on to your protagonist to see if this character will allow you to take the story in the direction you're most interested in.

For instance, in the following story Kit is currently the protagonist:

Fifteen-year-old Kit lives on the streets and steals cars for a living. He gets increasingly involved in a gang that wants to use him for more risky work. To begin with he's flattered by attention, glory and money, but soon realises they're exploiting him. When he tries to walk away, they come after him and he's trapped. He has to follow orders or be killed. He has no one else to turn to.

➤ What if you see the same basic premise from the perspective of other possible protagonists?

Twenty-two-year-old Ruby has been with the gang for many years and is desperate to get out. She sees her chance by involving Kit, only to realise she's doing to him what had been done to her. Ruby decides she has to help Kit as well as herself.

Forty-year-old Britt has been searching for the son she gave up for adoption as a baby. A private detective brings news of Kit. As Britt goes to find him, she witnesses Kit beating up an old man and stealing his car. She's not sure what to do. Does she want a son like this?

Fourteen-year-old Bobby grew up in the care home with Kit and always looked on him as a brother. Whatever Kit does, so does Bobby. When Kit runs away, so does Bobby – except that Bobby is found and brought back. Bobby tries to impress Kit by getting in with the gang and doing crazy stuff. But Bobby isn't good at what he does and inadvertently gets Kit into more danger.

Thirty-year-old Woady is the gang leader and has spent a lot of time building up operations. He won't be messed about, and though he sees potential in Kit, he also feels he's a threat, a contender for the throne. Woady decides the time has come to get rid of him, but Kit proves more wily than he first thought.

Twenty-year-old Lisa works at the children's home. She's in love with Kit and helped him escape. Kit occasionally sleeps at her place and she lets him, thinking one day he'll stay. She's found out and loses her job. Homeless, she turns to Kit but he isn't interested. Lisa is destitute, desperate and lost.

➤ How do you feel seeing these characters as protagonists? What stories come to mind? How does their perspective change the theme, plot or tone? How does it affect story mechanics? Which of their stories would you like to tell?

➤ Now, with one of your own stories, find at least five other possible protagonists, whether they're currently in the story or newly invented. Reflect on what happens to your story when you put each possible protagonist at the centre. How does it change? What themes and structures emerge? What hidden treasures? Which story do you most want to tell and why? Even if you stick with your original protagonist, you'll be clearer and stronger in your understanding of them.

Supermarket sweep

Observation is a key tool in the screenwriter's armoury. Watching, listening and absorbing the world around you will give you an understanding of how people operate and how the world they inhabit functions. Observation is a system of recognising, processing and reflecting; it's not simply an exercise in staring and eavesdropping! Screenwriters should approach observation as a method of deepening their understanding of characters, relationships and social behaviours.

There's nowhere better to observe people than out in public, especially in places where people routinely gather and interact. Supermarkets are great places for this because as well as bringing together a variety of types, they require people to undertake specific action. What things people buy, how they buy them, who they buy with, and everything in between offer rich potential for character development. As always, the key here is motivation – filling in the character's backstory.

> ➢ For this exercise, you need to visit a supermarket (or similar). Walk round and observe the people in there, shoppers and staff, and see if anyone stands out to you. Ask yourself, why do they stand out? What strikes you about them? Is it how they look, what they say, what they buy, or who they are with? Make some mental notes about this character.

> ➢ Now find another character and do the same. Ask dramatic questions about them, such as 'Who are they cooking for?' and 'What do they think about the prices?'

> ➢ When you get back home, take the people you've observed as a starting point for developing them into potential screen characters. What stories might they tell? What journeys might they go on? What happens if both characters are put into the same story?

> ➢ Try the exercise again, but this time in other communal settings: an office, a café, a bus stop, a museum, a pub or a train, for example.

Character building

Sometimes writers treat characters like mechanical pawns whose main task is to push the plot along. But characters have rights too! The more you treat them as authentic human beings, the more help they give to deepen emotion, clarify theme, direct structure and voice dialogue.

Character work creates plot ideas and solves story problems. By exploring characters, the story builds from the inside out and flows naturally, making it feel engaging and believable. You can never explore a character too much; it's rewarding, ongoing work that supports the story in so many ways.

CHARACTER PAST: BACKSTORY

Where a character comes from and what their past experiences are can have a big bearing on how they act and react in the present. Excavating a character's backstory isn't primarily about 'pop psychology' (e.g., they hate their life because they were bullied at school), but about mining the character so they feel rich and real. A writer has to know as much as possible about each character, in order for the story to come alive.

Knowing your character's past is not about generalities like their relation to their parents or where they went to school. Backstory is about finding necessary information to feed the story in the present. So if the story is about *a small family circus who tour villages in the summer and live in a cramped apartment in winter,* you may explore issues like: how long has the circus been working? How did they start? What kind of shows do they put on? Have they ever fallen out? Did they ever expand? What have past summer tours been like – successful or disastrous? How did they find their winter home? Where does the family come from? Are they from a line of circus folk? All this creates fertile ground for the present story to root and grow in.

➢ Choose three main characters from one of your stories. Write five relevant questions for each character's past. Choose one for each person that it feels vital to know more about. Write a first-person monologue for each character where they talk about that moment, in two different ways: first, write it as it happened, from their perspective of who they were then; second, write it from the present, as they remember it from who they are now. What are the differences between the perspectives? What do you learn about them?

CHARACTER PRESENT: ATTITUDES AND VALUES

A character isn't only the sum of their past but is also their essential self in the present. Their main values and attitudes can be explored by asking each character in the story a list of questions about themselves. By comparing the different characters' answers, further information is often revealed. Useful questions for this could be:

- What are their everyday habits?
- How would they describe themselves?
- How would others describe them?
- What's their worst fear?
- What's their secret longing?
- What makes them angry?
- What makes them laugh?
- What was the worst thing they ever did?
- What was the best thing they ever did?
- Who do they most want to be like, and why?

Once you've distinguished their main values and traits, you should dig deeper to hear what the characters have to say themselves. Writing first-person monologues is a powerful way to access a character's inner world, allowing them to say who they are and what they feel in their own words.

➤ Probe your characters further by writing a first-person monologue:

- From your main character's perspective on the morning of the day when the story begins.
- From your antagonist's perspective at the moment they first meet the protagonist.
- From the perspective of your protagonist's best friend or ally, at a moment when the protagonist most needs help.
- From all the main characters' points of view at each major turning point or moment of big decision in the story.

Though it sounds simple, this is one of the most powerful tools in screenwriting. It's recommended you use it as much as possible, with varied characters and story moments.

A creative portrait

Being creative means absorbing the world around you, making interesting interpretations of it, and putting these elements together to create fresh, original ideas. For example, you might be attracted to the personality of someone you meet, excited by the point of view of someone you overhear, or enamoured by the physical and spiritual environment that you find yourself in.

➢ This exercise is about building a creative portrait of a potential character by putting together a variety of elements that you've come across recently in your life. As it's a creative exercise, don't worry about forcing together a credible character; simply build the character by using individual elements that you're attracted to in different people.

➢ Think about people you've come across recently then build a character by putting together the following elements:

o Face: who has an interesting face? What does it say?

o Heart: who has a heart that has made an impression on you? What's it like?

o Body: have you encountered any surprising bodies recently?

o Hair: how might hair say something about someone? Do you know such a person?

o Voice: who says things in interesting ways? What's their perspective on life?

o Job: who have you met with a memorable job recently?

o Hopes: what does someone aspire to be or to have?

o Fears: what holds someone back?

➢ Now that you've built the skeleton framework of a character, have some fun by putting them into a variety of dramatic situations and letting them act and react. What do you learn about them? How does the portrait encourage or challenge their behaviour? Do any interesting story ideas emerge? Are you tempted to develop this character further?

Inside out

Once you've completed a certain amount of character work, you may feel you know them well. But sometimes you get stuck with a character, or put them in a box that's too tight or simple. Always allow characters to develop as the story develops. Maybe they'll surprise you and tell you more than you already knew. Characters aren't simply good or bad, black or white, so keep digging to create complex, rounded human beings. Allowing a character to keep growing can also give rise to interesting plot twists and surprises.

We can't deny who we essentially are, but along the way this must be stretched and tested. The character's essence stays the same, but the way their qualities engage with the story changes, helping both to create and solve problems. In this way, characters remain at the centre of plot and their essential abilities help them to grow and the story to unfold.

➢ Ask yourself what's your character's essential strength or skill. Write down how it currently manifests in the script: how is it shown, how does the character use it, how does it affect the story?

➢ Write at least fifteen ways that the same strength or skill could become a weakness or problem for your character.

➢ Look at your list and pick the five most interesting. How could they become part of the story? What would happen? How would it affect other characters? What could it lead to?

➢ Consider how to best use this new information to deepen the character and create surprising plot turns.

➢ Finally, brainstorm a list of fifteen ways their strength or skill can get them out of the problem it also created; how it can be put to use?

Consider this example:

> *Omar is an eight-year-old boy whose main strength is his curiosity. He loves to observe the world around him and see what's happening. He's a naive, happy child who more than anything wants to understand how things work.*

➢ With this in mind, how could his curiosity cause problems? For instance:

o He sticks his nose in where it doesn't belong and asks too many questions, revealing neighbours' private lives and making them angry.

o He puts his fingers into electrical sockets or gets too close to train tracks and finds himself in physical danger.

o He's easily led by his need to know, is readily distracted and suddenly finds himself lost and far away.

➢ In this way, story problems originate from the essence of the character. But the same trait can cause both problems and solutions, and exist both as weakness and strength. For instance, because of Omar's curiosity, he always looks further than the problem and does understand how things work, so his skill provides him with the idea of how he can resolve the problem.

➢ Now try the following:

> *Sonia is a deep-sea diver whose main strength is determination. She has battled her way through a tough education amid sexist colleagues, but never given up. Her determination has kept her alive and made her successful in her field.*

➢ In what ways could her determination become a weakness? Brainstorm five ways, then pick the one you like best. Look at the problems this can cause, and find at least three ways that her determination then creates a solution to this.

What's in a name?

Although this exercise is somewhat artificial, it does allow you a) to have fun with naming your characters and b) to free up your mind to creative possibilities that may eventually turn into something useful. So often we think we know a character but we don't express them well enough. This exercise allows all facets of a character to be considered, in a playful yet meaningful way.

➢ Take the name of a character you're working on and find an adjective or expression for each letter of their name that suits them well. For example, Harry is:

Honest

'Ard working

Reliable

Rigid

Young-at-heart

➢ Now go through the name and change one adjective or expression at a time, this time aiming to inject conflict or tension for a dramatic reversal that could create story potential. For example, this time Harry might be:

Hopeless

'Ard working

Reliable

Rigid

Young-at-heart

➢ How might the change open up fresh ideas for your character's story? In Harry's case, if he's hopeless then do we feel sorry for him? Or do we get annoyed by him? Or does it give him a specific challenge to try and undertake?

➢ Continue with this exercise, changing the next adjective or expression. For example:

Honest

Anti-immigration

Reliable

Rigid

Young-at-heart

➢ Create as wide a range of character and story possibilities as you can. You never know what ideas might surface . . .

Stepping into change

In most scripts characters aren't static. Though on some level they're always essentially themselves, physical events ensure that they constantly evolve. In a few stories, often tragedies, the protagonist doesn't change, failing to take the step they need to. But even here, although the character may not change, their story affects the audience, and it's the audience who changes and gains insight.

Some writers get stuck on a character's issue and simply re-state it throughout the story, instead of using it as a starting point and allowing them to change. A key way of deepening characters is to explore their journey through a story, to find what's revealed as they develop.

➢ Pick a character in your story. Write one or two sentences about where they are in the beginning, physically and emotionally. Do it again at each major turning point: inciting incident, end of Act One, mid-point, end of Act Two, biggest choice/battle, and end of Act Three. At each, clarify the major change in the character.

➢ Finally, summarise the character's journey and major change in one sentence. Do this with all main characters in your script. For example:

○ *Marja's a zookeeper. She lives alone – apart from four cats and two dogs. Her only friends are animals, and she's great at talking with them. She's not good at talking to people, who she finds difficult and complex.*

○ *One day Adam, a new trainer, begins at the zoo, and challenges Marja's way of working. She's too soft, he says. Marja gets angry but can't find the right words to stand up for what she believes in.*

○ *Marja's angry with Adam and hates working with him. She badmouths him to her boss, but this backfires. At the end of Act One, she's demoted and forced to become Adam's assistant.*

○ *During Act Two, Marja hates the way Adam orders the animals around. She feels he has no understanding. She tries to sabotage his job and gets the animals to work with her against Adam.*

○ *At the midpoint, one of the gorillas misunderstands Marja's instructions and hurts Adam badly in an attempt to scare him. Adam's taken to hospital and Marja gets scared. She feels guilty and visits him. As he can't speak, she uses animal communication with him and finds to her amazement that they have a good time together.*

○ *At the end of Act Two, Marja and Adam have fallen in love. He's discharged from hospital, but as he comes back into the human world, Marja refuses to have anything more to do with him. She thinks she's made a mistake and hands in her notice.*

○ *Her biggest choice is when one of the monkeys falls ill and Adam tells her they need her help. She has to come back and work with Adam to save the monkey. As she does so, she realises how Adam has changed and wants to learn from her about animal communication.*

○ *At the end of Act Three, Marja and Adam decide to move in together, but to a much bigger place – to house their ever-growing family of animal friends.*

Marja's journey is about a shy silent girl who develops different ways to speak and communicate. Her major change is daring to come out from her world and begin to form human relationships.

Lost baggage

Characters can sometimes seem flat and unappealing, even difficult to write, because they've not been developed sufficiently. Their backstory might not have been explored enough to give them a believable and tangible existence. This will have a direct effect on many things, such as the way they speak, how they react to situations and how they operate in groups and it will have a crucial effect on the character's dramatic motive. If you know your character well enough to show us why they do what they do, you're giving enough credible motivation to justify the actions. This has an important impact on the audience's engagement with the character, and the function or purpose of the story.

Finding out about a character's past can have a positive impact on how you construct their story and, in doing this, create deeper levels of engagement between the character and the audience.

➤ Take the following scenarios and ask yourself questions to get to the bottom of why the characters act as they do. From this, consider whether there's mileage in their reasons to develop a full story – if finding out about a character's 'baggage,' and what they need to do with it can open up possibilities for exciting and engaging screenplays.

○ *Paul, a sixteen-year-old boy, doesn't want to go on holiday with his family this year.*

○ *Sheila, a forty-year-old air hostess, refuses to upgrade a passenger whose in-flight entertainment system isn't working properly.*

○ *Ryan, a city banker, really wants to get a bus rather than a train to the seaside next weekend.*

○ *Samuel, a PhD student, wants to really spoil his boyfriend on Valentine's Day.*

○ *Kazia, a mother with three children, has the urge to contact an old flame for the first time in ten years.*

➤ Think of at least ten possible reasons why each character does or feels the above, finding where possible different types of baggage. If an idea appeals to you, plot the character's journey with the situation above as the first scene of the screenplay. What would happen next?

Motivating action

Characters are revealed not only by who they are and what they say, but also by what they do. Actions, reactions and decisions all reveal a character and what's important to them. By seeing a character choose a certain path, the audience can sense their motivation and get a deeper understanding of them.

Thus, who we are is not only what we do, but also what we choose. If the choice is easy, it doesn't tell you much, but if it's a hard choice the character is really forced to show what's most important to them. So through these choices inner values and emotions are exposed.

➢ Pick a character who's facing a moment of decision. Brainstorm a list of at least ten other choices that the character could make in this moment. Think about what each choice tells you about the character, what it could mean for them, and how it would affect their character development as well as the story as a whole. Compare this character's choice with another character's in the same situation. What do their different decisions show you about their different characters?

It's also important to remember that the same physical choice can be motivated by different wants or needs. In this way a writer can play with audience expectation and understanding, and reveal different sides of a character at different times.

➢ Pick the same character at the same moment of decision. Now brainstorm a list of at least ten different reasons for why they took this decision. Push yourself to consider all sorts of things, even if they don't feel as though they fit. Look at all the reasons to see what they reveal about the character, and what kind of dramatic pressure and secrets each reason can create.

For example:

➢ *Roy only has enough money to either get a drink or get the bus home. What are his choices?*

  o *He buys a drink and walks home.*

  o *He buys a drink and tries to hitch a lift.*

  o *He buys a drink and sleeps in a bush.*

  o *He stands outside the pub, longingly watching the people indoors before he gets the bus home.*

  o *He stands outside the pub and begs people for money as they go in.*

  o *He chats up women or tells funny stories to get people to buy him drinks.*

  o *He steals money from drunk people or from the tips on the bar.*

  o *He asks the owner if he can get drinks on credit. She says no but he can unblock the toilets and get a free drink.*

  o *He decides he's had enough of drinking and never wants to go home again, and spends the money on a ticket out of here.*

➢ *Roy decides to spend his last money on drink and sleep in a bush. What are his reasons?*

  o *He was too drunk to care.*

  o *He'd been thrown out of his girlfriend's flat and had nowhere to go.*

  o *He loves to sleep outdoors under the stars.*

  o *He lives for today and doesn't worry about tomorrow.*

  o *He was so depressed he couldn't think further than the next drink.*

  o *He knew his father would beat him if he came home drunk.*

  o *He's celebrating his new job and knows he'll soon get more money.*

Composing lists of motivations and decisions can also help to create a chain of events where the character starts with the easiest choice (the path of least resistance) and, when that doesn't work, has to try something harder, then even more so. With the example above, Roy could start by begging, then trying to chat up a woman with no success, and finally by stealing the money he wants. Through such action–reaction–decision chains, the character is revealed in depth as they struggle with a problem and are continually forced to choose what to do.

Public and private spheres

What makes characters rich, interesting and intriguing is not just how they behave, but how they do so in different environments and circumstances. Just like real-life people, screen characters have different 'comfort zones' and various masks they wear depending on the given situation. As well as adding complexity to a character, this also opens up possibilities for story potential. For example, *if Parvinder finds it difficult to express herself at school but is very happy to express herself at home,* we begin to wonder why. In this way we actively seek back-story and character motivation that may then organically transform into an exciting and viable storyline.

The purpose of this exercise is to probe a character that you're currently developing in order to release story potential, and by considering the idea of public vs private, explore the possible tension and conflict that might exist in their inner fabric.

➢ Take your character and write down five private places you might find them in. You might already have an idea of some, such as their house or their partner's house. When you have the list, write next to each place three adjectives that describe how your character feels when they're in that location. Try to vary the adjectives with each location, thinking carefully what it is about that place that makes them feel in such a way.

➢ Now do the same but for the public places you might find your character in. Think about how they might feel differently from when they're in the private places, and if so, how differently?

➢ Are there any surprising differences in how your character feels between public and private spheres? What are they? If there are major differences, what might this say about your character? What is it about each place that creates such feelings (adjectives)? Is there any mileage here for exploring how and why the differences have come about?

➢ Now take two of the private places and their adjectives away from the character. How might your character react to this? Which adjectives are you now left with, and which ones have been taken away? How might the character try and replace the feelings brought about by those two private places? Is there a possibility of the character trying to change one or more of the public places to replace those lost feelings? If so, what happens when public and private collide, and how does the character cope with this?

5 Shaping relationships

When developing characters, it's not only the individual that's key but the relationships they're in. A character on their own can only show us so much, whereas a character in relation to others will provide information about emotions, attitudes, values, power, fears and hopes. Although characters are essentially nearly always themselves, they do show different sides when they're with different people, and let the audience see for themselves the complexity and depth of the story without having to have it spelt out.

Relationships are important both as dramatic and thematic fuel. By causing conflicts, they force characters to show what they want, challenge them in their arc, and make them act and react to events going on around them. If crafted with care, relationships can also vibrate with deeper thematic meaning, using specific dramatic functions related to the central character journey or theme. Relationships tell us about many aspects of the world we live in and about the values of the writer, and they echo the audience's hopes and fears.

This chapter will help you to develop a web of relationships that will reveal deeper meaning and purpose behind the stories that you're writing. After you've explored your characters in depth through the exercises in Chapter 4, take time to explore the various relationships that they bring with them and find out how they can work as a powerful storytelling tool.

The odd couple

In traditional Western narrative, the main conflict lies between protagonist and antagonist. Simply put, the protagonist seeks something and the antagonist makes it difficult to get. Even when going beyond this quintessential 'hero–villain' model, it's highly likely the story will be made up of central relationships with characters creating problems for one another. This exercise is valuable for any relationship where characters oppose each other, to whatever degree.

The essential concern in such relationships is finding the right protagonist–antagonist pairing. Chapter 4 offered an exercise in choosing the best protagonist; now that's set, central dramatic relationships have to be established. The best antagonist may seem obvious, but it's always rewarding to explore further to find if they are the most relevant choice and to define their dramatic function.

By taking time to find the right central relationships, the story almost creates itself. Different antagonists for the same protagonist will naturally create different themes and journeys through the story. By choosing the right antagonist, you'll take a huge step toward shaping the essential heart of the script. If you want the story to say one thing, but choose an antagonist that makes it say another, it'll be difficult to marry the two. Understanding more about central relationships will help you see if you're really telling the story you think you are.

On a structural level, the right antagonist creates the obstacles and challenges that take the protagonist through their journey to where they need to go. Without the antagonist, they would be stuck in their 'want' and never reach their necessary 'need'.

➢ To explore this further, choose one of the following protagonists:

> *Dot, seventy-six, is a bored widow with a lot of life left in her. She dreams of new adventures, but is afraid of dishonouring her dead husband's memory.*

> *Ahmed, seventeen, works in a petrol station. He is a bit of a dreamer and hopelessly in love with a beautiful girl who comes in every morning to buy coffee.*

> *Jimmy, fifty, is a school janitor. He feels ignored and all he really wants is to be respected, noticed and given credit for how hard he works.*

➢ Create five possible antagonists for the one chosen protagonist. Make them as different as possible, using a variety of genres or styles.

➢ Think about:

   o Their values, skills, strengths and weaknesses.

   o Different ways and reasons they can cause problems in the story.

   o What relationship they can have to the protagonist.

➢ Look at what happens to the story when each antagonist is used. What's the effect, what story is suggested by each character-pairing? Choose a final antagonist from the list, considering who'll help to shape the most appropriate protagonist journey.

➢ Try this with one of your own stories, going beyond what you already have. Brainstorm at least five new possible antagonists, and see what effect it'll have on your narrative.

Finding the right antagonist

As well as providing the most obvious form of conflict, there's a strange connectivity between protagonist and antagonist in that they desperately rely on each other for the narrative to function. Although the protagonist may actively try to defeat the antagonist, they actually have a lot to thank them for. This is because of the emotional journey they're allowed to undergo as a result of the tumultuous path laid out for them.

As it's so important to find the right antagonist, the figure who will offer conflict and connection, this exercise will help you to think further about this dramatically dependent pairing.

➢ With each of the following protagonists, make a list of five things they wouldn't want to do, and five worlds they wouldn't want to inhabit. Think about what their implied arc might be, and make your choices according to what would be difficult for them, yet at the same time enable their character arc.

   o Grace, a six-year-old beauty pageant queen who's vying for her third crown.

   o Simon, a fifteen-year-old up-and-coming fishing star who skives off school.

- o Cesar, a twenty-five-year-old trainee pilot working for a budget airline.

- o Sharon, a forty-year-old virgin who's recently lost her job.

- o Brenda, a sixty-five-year-old petty criminal who's just been released from a short stint in prison.

➤ Now write five antagonists for each character based on your ideas. Think carefully about what the antagonists would bring to the story, for both plot and world. How do the antagonists represent what the protagonist really doesn't want to do? How do they embody the world that doesn't want to be inhabited?

➤ When you have five antagonists for each character, combine their personality traits to make one 'bigger and better' antagonist. How does this antagonist now represent everything the protagonist doesn't want to do and everywhere they don't want to be?

Antagonist as thematic driver

An antagonist isn't there simply to create conflict and make life difficult for the protagonist; the true purpose of an antagonist is to offer the kind of obstacles that will propel the protagonist through their essential journey. They force the protagonist to address the issues they need to face in order to move through the thematic landscape of the story. If you take the time to find the right antagonist, you'll find that the theme will be revealed in greater depth and that you will be able to avoid the obvious and over-familiar.

➤ This exercise will help you to consider what happens when different antagonists are combined with the same protagonist, and what the natural storytelling and thematic possibilities become when two characters meet.

Here's the protagonist:

Margie's fifty-eight. She's a gardener with a love of plants but a mean streak when it comes to humans. She hates children as they make a mess of the public gardens she manages. At home she dreams of creating new plant hybrids that will make her famous and allow her well-hidden love of life to shine. She's terrified of losing her job as it's the only thing in her life that gives her value.

These are three possible antagonists:

Robert is eight years old. He's unhappy at school and lives with his father, who doesn't have enough time for him because he has to work hard to earn money. Robert likes to look at life close up and analyse how it works, but he's not good at applying this information to human lives. He's not interested in having friends, and doesn't care who knows it.

Anne is twenty-three. She's a brilliant new gardener employed to work with Margie in the parks. Anne has a lot of new ideas and huge enthusiasm. She's warm and easy and everyone seems to love her. She dreams of travelling to the ends of the earth and discovering long-lost ancient plants with medicinal value.

Jim is fifty-five, and Margie's recently widowed brother. Jim had a happy, steady life with his wife of thirty years but now he feels lost. He insists on coming to live with Margie until he gets back on his feet, since he can't bear to be alone. He was once an excellent mechanic but has lost his touch and isn't interested in getting it back. He just wants to talk about old times, and spends a lot of time by his wife's grave, tending it lovingly.

➢ Put Margie together with each antagonist, one at a time, and write 100 words on what happens. What kind of stories and situations develop? What different aspects of the protagonist's story do they bring out? Does the theme change? When you've written all three, compare and contrast the different versions of your protagonist's possible journey. Which do you like best? Why? What does it teach you about the function of the antagonist as a thematic driver for the protagonist?

The third party

The catalyst or 'inciting incident' of many screenplays is the arrival of a character whose function is to bring a new perspective to the ordinary world experienced by the main characters, be it positive or negative. This character begins to challenge 'the norm' and disrupt the existing relationships the audience has seen so far. For characters already established, this can mean a whole host of fraught, tense yet potentially exciting times ahead.

The creative screenwriter

➤ Choose two characters that you're working on or that you know, preferably a couple or close friends. Think carefully about their relationship, and write notes about it. It might be helpful to consider the following:

  ○ How long have they known each other?
  ○ How do they feel about each other?
  ○ Do both know how each of them feels about the other?
  ○ What have they done together?
  ○ What haven't they done together?
  ○ If they could change one thing about the other, what would it be?

➤ Put them into a situation where they're together in a place they're familiar with: at home, in a restaurant, on a regular journey, etc. Sketch out a scene about this, but no longer than a page.

➤ Now introduce a third character who will in some way (positive or negative) alter their relationship. Choose someone who actually knows the characters, or make the character up; either way, think carefully about who this person is and what they might bring to the relationship and situation.

➤ Continue to write the scene, but with the third person arriving and affecting it. Don't think too prescriptively – just allow the scene to flow and the relationship to develop.

➤ Once you've done this, look back at the scene and analyse what's been going on. What was the relationship like before the third party arrived? How did their arrival affect the scene? How has the initial relationship changed, and why? Were there any interesting power shifts? Did the tone change? How do all three characters feel at the end of the scene? What new dramatic possibilities have been created? Where might it go from here?

➤ Finally, think about a screenplay you've written to see if bringing in one or more characters might add something fresh. Is there an interesting character who could come in and disrupt the normality, either as an inciting incident to the whole story or as a catalyst to a specific scene?

Weaving webs

Character relationships often create a web upon which story and structure rest. If you clarify all key relationships, how they work and what's at stake in each, it's easier to see how and where the story needs to be improved.

> *Rosemary has an affair with Louisa. Her teenage children Matt and Helena find out and aren't happy. They move to live with their dad, Greg.*

➢ What's the web of relationships in this premise?

> *Rosemary and Louisa love each other and feel happier than they've ever been. Rosemary finds Helena difficult and gets easily annoyed with her. She gets along better with Matt, who's sober and sensible, and asks him for help to mediate with Helena. She likes Greg a lot and gets on with him like a brother.*

> *Helena and Louisa have always had a special relationship. Helena feels she can talk to Louisa about all the things she could never tell her mother. Because she felt Louisa was a special friend, she feels betrayed by the love affair. Helena gets along well with her younger brother, bosses him around but also admires him for his calm. Helena thinks Greg should stand up to her mum. She's angry with Rosemary but secretly misses her, and is unhappy living with Greg.*

> *Matt is a peacemaker and finds conflict upsetting. He really likes his mum and his dad and listens to both, which sometimes makes him confused. Louisa makes him nervous because he's not sure where she fits in. Helena is someone who tells him exciting stories and is the daredevil he knows he'll never be.*

> *Louisa is mixed up by the affair. Though she loves Rosemary, she feels guilty at the pain it causes Helena. She tries to have secret talks with Helena, whom she likes very much. She's never quite sure how to talk to Matt. She finds Greg a pleasant, kind man who gives in too easily to Rosemary, and wonders if this is how Rosemary will end up treating her too.*

➢ By looking at the main interconnected relationships, a myriad stories and perspectives come to light. Characters become more rounded, and the different ways they affect each other become clear. By seeing a character in relation to others, their different sides are revealed and they become more complex, interesting and human. This is an excellent way to work, as it avoids characters becoming too clichéd or simplistic. It's also a useful exercise at the beginning of development as it offers new pathways and possibilities to enrich both plot and emotional life of the story.

➤ Try it with one of your own scripts. Choose five or six main characters and, as in the example above, write out their feelings, thoughts, attitudes and behaviours in relation to a variety of different relationships in the story. Write as much as you can for each relationship, to discover things you don't know.

➤ Read through all the relationship strands and see how they affect each other. Draw a map to get a clearer picture of how they relate, and how pulling on one of the strands will automatically affect the others. How can you use this newfound knowledge to tell the story in a more intricate way?

Family values

Relationships are not static; like a screenplay narrative itself, they move, morph, peak and trough. Sometimes revelations in a plot alter relationships drastically, resulting in changing allegiances. This is very interesting for an audience, who will try and make sense of the shifting relationship patterns that they see. To explore the core of this, using conflict to test relationships in times of crisis can be effective.

➤ Take the characters of mother, father and son. Write a scene in which the son reveals something unexpected to his mother and father – a secret, a truth, etc. You decide what. Start the scene with the revelation and initially let it play out with the mother accepting or dealing with it and the father denying it.

➤ Now write a second version of the scene, this time changing a dynamic of the relationship. The scene should start in the same place, but needs to move in a different direction. Consider, for example:

   o   What if the mother starts to deny it?

   o   How might the father learn to accept it?

- ○ What if the son wishes he hadn't revealed it?
- ○ What if mother and father pledge allegiance together, against the son?
- ○ What if the revelation pushes mother and father apart?

➤ Once you've done this exercise, make some notes about the changes in the characters' relationships. What happened? What didn't happen? Why did a change take place? How did the characters respond to change? Which changes did you like? What emotions did they capture?

➤ Explore how this change in the family's relationships might be played out over the course of a whole screenplay. What might the story be? How would you tell it? At which point might the scene above come into the screenplay? Write a story outline in roughly 250 words, and block out the key structural points that relate to the changing relationships.

A matter of perspective

What happens in a story always depends on whose eyes it's seen through. Different characters experience the same event in different ways, depending on where they are, who they are and what they want. You can learn a lot about the story by seeing the same situation from different perspectives. Try these variations:

➤ Pick a key moment in your story. Choose three to five characters who will in some way be affected by this moment. Write a monologue in first person for each character, where they talk about the moment. Maybe they experience it first hand, maybe they were told about it, maybe they found out another way. Let them tell you about their feelings, thoughts and personal perspective of this moment.

➤ Pick an event in the backstory that has relevance for the present story. Choose three to five characters who were affected by it – maybe they were part of it, maybe someone they're close to was affected, maybe it influenced future events now affecting them. Write a first-person monologue for each in which they talk about the event. Write both from the perspective of the past, as it happened, and as they remember it now.

> Pick a key relationship in your story, maybe between lovers, family, friends or colleagues. Write first-person monologues for every person involved in the relationship, in which they divulge thoughts and feelings about the other(s) in it. Don't think or plan too much, just write and see what comes. This will help you go more deeply into a relationship and see different aspects, giving more rounded characters and satisfying emotional complexity.

> Once you've written a number of monologues about an event or relationship, read and compare them. What do you learn about the characters and their relationships? What more can you find by seeing the monologues in relation to each other? How might you use this information dramatically in the script?

Generating perspective

Some screenplays deliberately play around with perspective and the 'unreliable narrator', but even traditional screenplays show some aspect of alternative character viewpoints. Knowing a character's perspective helps to drive a scene's direction, and when coupled with alternative perspectives from other characters creates dramatic conflict and heightened audience engagement. It's therefore important to know a character's perspective towards a given situation. You might know this already, through carefully planned backstory, or it might develop organically as the writing of the screenplay progresses.

> Choose a situation you've experienced recently – something that's been a big event, either literally or emotionally. Write non-stop about this for about ten minutes, in the form of a first-person monologue. Write from your perspective: how do you feel about the situation? What effect has it had on you?

> Read through the completed monologue and highlight the parts that stand out as generating the strongest perspective: emotive words and phrases, etc. Pull all of this together and evaluate the presented perspective. What's emerged from the monologue? Which emotions stand out? Does the language give a clear sense of perspective?

> Finally, write a scene where you (as a character) try to convince someone else who's been involved in the situation (also as a character)

of your perspective. How do you express yourself as a character? What conflicts and tensions arise from the other person? How do you overcome them and continue trying to persuade? Structurally, how does the scene begin and end, and how does this support your perspective? Does anyone win in the end?

Listening out for relationships

At certain times in the writing process it can be very helpful to get outside input and inspiration, to see things you've not thought of, get out of your own head and find new sides to characters. This can be particularly good when you get stuck or just can't find a way to make a relationship work well enough.

➢ Go to a public place such as a café, park, swimming pool or bus. While being inconspicuous and respectful, observe and listen to a conversation between two people there. Look out for different kinds of relationships to see what they tell you about power, emotion, connection, conflict and desire:

o Children

o Old people

o Women speaking together or men speaking together

o Friends

o Parent and child

o Boss and worker

➢ Listen to what they say, how they say it, how they are with each other, what they do. What's the essence of their relationship (status, power, affection, anger, etc.)? How is it expressed? What's not being said? Do they pay attention to each other? Do they want to be together? Is there balance or imbalance between them?

➢ Write down what you learn about people in relationships and consider how to use it to enrich a story or create new scenes.

Ensembles

Certain stories centre on a group of key people rather than on a main protagonist. Ensemble films or TV series explore a theme from different perspectives, allowing a world to form where each person's understanding is of roughly equal value. By placing characters in relation to each other in this marked way, the story is told through their alliances and allegiances. The whole thus created can explore a theme or situation in a different way from the single protagonist narrative.

An ensemble can in itself be seen as the central character, and its form has a strong effect on the script. The type of characters chosen and the way they mix and connect is integral to shaping theme, tone and plot. The relationships within the ensemble create the dramatic possibilities for the story, so it's important to choose ensemble members well.

➢ Find a film that focuses its story on a group of characters. Watch it and write down all main members of the ensemble.

➢ Distinguish the main dramatic function of each member. For example, 'wild and wants action', 'looks after everyone else', 'angry and lost' or 'searches for the truth'. Look at the list of dramatic functions and consider how each relates to the theme or central dramatic question of the story.

➢ Why have these particular characters been chosen to make up the ensemble? Look at how they interrelate and create a map of the different relationships, and how they fit together.

➢ Now create your own ensemble. Considering theme, tone and genre, which eight characters would be useful as a group for the following premise?

A group of colleagues hike through a mountain range to prove who'll be most worthy of an upcoming promotion.

➢ Experiment with different kinds of character and different combinations to see how the ensemble changes and what effect it has on the story. What happens if a character disappears or dies? What happens to the group? How do the members react? What functions need to be fulfilled by others? What does this tell you about the purpose of the individual in the group?

Absent friends

Some of the best characters in a story can be absent ones. They may not literally be on screen, but still have a powerful influence on what happens. Using the example from the previous exercise, the boss may not physically feature in the script, but her role in the narrative is essential and the way she affects it is crucial. Sometimes the audience never meets a character but they hear about them. Such absent characters must also be explored by the writer, to know who they are and what relationship they have to the main cast.

➤ Using your ensemble members from the previous exercise, write first-person monologues from each about their boss. How do they feel about her? What relationship do they have with her? What threats or opportunities does she pose for them? What do you learn about the boss from how other people see her and talk about her?

➤ Using the same premise, come up with at least three other kinds of character that could be absent from the physical plot but play an important part thematically or emotionally. Think of how they could be used and what kind of relationships they'd have to the different people in the ensemble.

➤ Analyse one of your own stories to see what possible absent characters there are that might influence the story. Explore their personalities and relationships with the main protagonists. How might you make use of them?

6 Designing structure

Structure refers to the architecture of a script; essentially, how story elements are put into place on the page. The order in which information is given to an audience determines their emotional response to the script, whether tension, surprise, empathy, anger, hope.

At first a story may seem to have an obvious shape, but that's only an initial suggestion. The same idea can be told in many different ways and for many different effects, so working with structure is a key part of discovering how best to express a story. Designing a finely tuned structure is like playing music – plucking at the heartstrings of the audience to create the right emotion.

Three-act structure has become a strong tradition within Western screenwriting theory and practice, and there's much to gain by learning about this. However, it should be viewed as a creative not a rigid endeavour; structure is about finding a form that works, not a formula that has to be followed. Therefore this chapter will cover some of the essentials of classic structure and how it can become a writer's best friend.

Like architecture, screenwriting works best when a screenplay is developed from the inside out, starting with the foundations and the skeleton and then adding the more colourful details later. To this end, further structure-focused exercises can be found in Chapter 16.

Structuring the emotional journey

At the heart of most screenplays is a clear character arc – an emotional journey that the protagonist travels, from some kind of lack to some kind of fulfilment. Although the most obvious thing when watching a film or TV drama may be its plot, often what is most important is its emotional journey. This is because it creates responses in the audience as well as the characters, and leaves them with a strong feeling about the underlying themes and meanings of the drama. So when structuring a script it's really important to think of the plot as a physical representation of the emotional journey; in other words, you orchestrate the emotion in the audience by plotting the action in relevant ways. This ensures that each time the action moves on, so does the character arc. The physical journey and emotional journey are intertwined as one, and need to function with and for each other.

> Choose a film or TV drama that you're familiar with and write a short summary of what you think it's about – both thematically and, for the character, emotionally. Then write a short summary of its plot and overall dramatic structure. Use broad brushstrokes rather than fine detail.

> Now revisit the drama and undertake a closer analysis of how it's plotted. As you watch, make notes about key moments of action and dramatic turning points. Step back from the analysis and think about why the plot has been structured in this way to bring out the character's emotional journey. Try to draw parallels between the physical action and the emotional arc. Is it clear how the action serves the emotion? Are the key turning points imbued with character development? Does the structure work to tease out the underlying themes?

> Now think about a screenplay you're working on. Summarise what you think it's about, thematically and emotionally. It's a good idea to consider what you want the audience to feel for the story and characters. Analyse the screenplay's structure and whether it's designed to bring out the themes. Is there a clear connection between the physical and emotional journey? Do the key turning points embed action and emotion? Might there be more effective ways to structure the emotional journey?

Character arc as structure

To build further on the relationship between character and plot, it's possible to ask a set of character questions where the answers come to provide the narrative structure. In this way the emphasis remains on the emotional reality of the character, rather than on fulfilling a series of formal structural elements.

➢ Pick a protagonist you have or are creating and ask:

- ○ What does their everyday life look like?

- ○ What's their main problem and what do they want?

- ○ What happens to disrupt the normal state of affairs? How do they react to this?

- ○ What does the character decide to do that will take them on to a new path? What's their plan? What do they want now?

- ○ What happens to them as they move in this new world? Who do they meet? What do they have to do? What do they begin to learn?

- ○ How do they respond to challenges and problems that arise? How do they begin to change? How does their plan change?

- ○ What do they have to do to get what they want? Who do they face?

- ○ How does it go wrong? What is the worst moment in their journey?

- ○ How do they recover from failure or hopelessness?

- ○ What's their hardest choice? What do they give up? What do they have to fight for? How does it change them?

- ○ What's their life like after all this? What do they want now? What have they learned in the end?

➢ By asking these questions in this order, a clear narrative will emerge. Compare your answers to the script structure you currently have, and how you might re-structure using the order of the questions. Not all stories follow this classical structure, but they're good questions to explore, to see what you may have missed when plotting the journey of your protagonist.

Chain reaction

A story doesn't only consist of events, it also needs emotion. How characters react to what happens is just as important as their actions. A good way to chart story structure is to locate *Action–Reaction–Decision* chains: something happens; it makes someone feel something; they make a decision based on it. This in turn causes new action, new reaction, new decisions; and so it goes on. By thinking in this way, the writer works from the inside out. Rather than imposing a 'correct' model on to the story, you look at what's happening and how characters feel about it, and let the structure build from the movement. This also creates a natural feeling of cause and effect which makes the plot feel more authentic and connective.

➢ Use the following premise to create *Action–Reaction–Decision* chains:

> *Theodore is a computer expert who's created software which allows users to stop normal time and enter a universe without stress or pressure. Number 1 test pilot Laura tries it out but disappears and never comes back.*

➢ What's Theodore's reaction? Is he frightened he did something wrong, is he angry with Laura? Does he miss her, or is he excited he's discovered something truly new? It all depends on his character. If he's frightened, what would his next action be, based on this? What decision would he come to? Write out a series of concise *Action–Reaction–Decision* chains related to this. What do you learn about how sequences are created and how events fit together and fuse?

➢ Now look at your own script and try to locate *Action–Reaction–Decision* chains. Are there many? Do you need more? How can you encourage a natural development of actions and reactions? Where will it take you?

Inciting incidents

An 'inciting incident' sets the story in motion and catalyses the plot, as well as essentially reminding the audience of the protagonist's dramatic problem and what they need to achieve. It thus becomes a major structural point for deepening and/or clarifying the character arc as well as triggering the rest of the plot. It's a moment that needs to take the character physically in the right direction towards the goal of their inner journey, as well as emotionally to embody the complications that will ensure this character growth.

➢ With each of the following protagonists, think of at least five inciting incidents that would propel their story. Create inciting incidents that will catalyse both a physical and an emotional journey – by all means thinking 'big' in plot terms, but also considering the core emotional journey.

  ○ *Dwaine's a newly qualified policeman. He's doing the usual 'petty crime' jobs, but craves more action. He's keen to impress his mother, who single-handedly raised him and made him the good citizen he is.*

  ○ *Zainab works as a train driver. She's almost reaching retirement age when she'll be forced to step down from her position. She can't stand the thought of being stuck at home with her husband.*

  ○ *Charlie's married but has secretly been seeing men behind his wife's back. He doesn't think he's gay, but likes the thrill of being with the same sex. He always avoids his wife's desires to try for a baby.*

➢ Considering the five possible inciting incidents for each protagonist, what kind of stories do you find? Does each one give a different character arc? Does each one suggest a different genre? If you had to put them in order of emotional impact, which would come out on top? Which ones speak to you most, and why?

➢ Now go back to the 'inciting incident' moment of a screenplay you're working on and assess whether or not it will effectively lead the character in the right direction, both physically and emotionally. What happens in the inciting incident? Does it embody strong action and deep emotion? Is it relevant to the protagonist and their journey? Is it appropriate to the story you're trying to tell?

All change

A turning point is a moment in a story when everything changes. The character can no longer return to the way things were but is forced to act and go further than they've gone before. Turning points are excellent dramatic fuel and an effective way to structure a script and work out the story. Since they feed change, turning points also ensure that a script naturally advances rather than gets stuck in the same beat.

Usually turning points come as the result of a character's action, reaction or decision. However, sometimes they impose themselves on the character from an outside agent. At the inciting incident and the midpoint, something usually happens that's out of the character's control, and they have to decide how to react and respond. Wherever it comes from, the trick with turning points is to really allow major change to happen – to dare your characters to step into unknown territory and move out of your own writing comfort zone.

> ➢ Create five possible turning points for the following situation. What could turn it on its head, change everything and force the character to take decisions and action?
>
> *Bojan grows roses. He's put all his money, heart and soul into creating the most beautiful garden and feels like he's living in paradise.*

> ➢ How do different turning points lead the story in different directions? What story structure does each suggest? How do they affect genre and theme?

> ➢ Now define five to seven major turning points in your current script. Write them out in order. Do they connect and create a natural flow? Do they provoke enough change in the character's situation? What other turning points could there be?

Planning the plan

Another way of approaching structure is to look at characters' plans. What do they want to do? How do they think they're going to get it? What do they have to achieve? How are they stopped or helped? Usually as a script develops a character has a plan which they try to fulfil. As it's thwarted, they have to come up with a new plan. New obstacles stop them and once again they have to revise their plan of action.

Working with plans is an excellent way to manage plot as it necessarily involves actions, reactions and decisions. The character tries to achieve something but it doesn't go according to plan. Therefore they have to constantly change, which gives dynamic energy to the script. Each turning point forces the character to amend their plan, so it's good to analyse how plans change after each major step. This will give a sense of direction to the narrative and how it needs to move until the next big road block comes into view.

➢ Look at the following premise. Come up with a specific concrete plan for how the protagonist can achieve her objective:

  Serena wants to discover gold.

➢ Write a paragraph that shows Serena's initial plan: how to start, what she needs to do, what she hopes will happen, how she'll execute it.

➢ Now find one point in her plan where she encounters a big obstacle. What is it and how does it stop her or thwart her plan? Be specific. How does it affect her? How does she have to change or revise her plan? What does her new plan consist of? Write a paragraph with as much detail as you can. Then find another obstacle to this new plan, and see how it has to change.

➢ Now choose one of your own stories and analyse the main character's plan/s. See what stops the plan/s being fulfilled and how it's forced to change. Go through the whole script and write an overview of how plans are executed, stopped, and changed. This movement will help you see where you need a clearer direction or more drama.

Plans can create ever-deepening plot structures as one character's plan comes up against another's. It's very useful to map out all major character plans in a story and see how they relate to and impose on each another.

Deepening the problem

The point of classic storytelling structure is to help the journey move forward. Sometimes writers get stuck with the initial problem instead of progressing it. The guidelines of three-act structure can help writers check that they're developing the story enough, instead of treading water. One way is to look at how you can deepen the problem at the heart of the story.

> ➤ Instead of brainstorming ways to come into conflict, this exercise deepens the core question by seeing how each step develops the central issue that will eventually lead to a thematic resolution.

> *Alexia and Paul are setting out for a summer road trip backpacking across South America.*

> ➤ If the central dramatic question is *Will their relationship survive?*, a gradual deepening of the theme could result in this structure:

> o *Before they start, they bicker about travel plans.*

> o *They settle on Paul's plan. Alexia pretends to be happy but isn't.*

> o *As they travel, Alexia makes new friends and Paul feels threatened.*

> o *They argue, revealing their different reasons for making the trip.*

> o *Alexia goes off with her new friends on their journey.*

> o *Angry and lost, Paul makes plans to go home early.*

> o *He gets a call saying Alexia is missing and her parents are frantic.*

> o *He decides to try and find her, feeling his love for her again* (etc.).

> ➤ Try this with the same premise but create a structure that will deepen the following new central dramatic question:

> *How will the environmental disaster they encounter change them and their view of the world?*

Building plot and clarifying structure through focusing on the problem at the heart of the story will create scripts with a solid core and authentic journey. This will help the writer to understand what they're writing about and where the story needs to go.

Rising action

The classic way to enable a story to move forward is to create complications – so that not only does a character have an objective, they also have problems achieving it. However, the problem can't stay the same through the story; it has to change as characters act and react to it.

Rising action refers to the way that the problem not only changes or deepens on a thematic level, but gets worse on a surface-plot level. In a way you could look at it as a training programme: as the character gets more determined and clear, they face more challenging obstacles.

Using rising action helps to maintain high tension and temperature, and stops a story becoming slack. But rising action isn't about action for its own sake. A well-structured curve of ever-worsening problems can help a character get to where they need to go, learn what they need to learn and show what they care about. As always, character and structure are closely entwined.

➢ Using the premise from 'What's the Problem?' in Chapter 3, look at these ways to create a sense of rising action.

> *Mickey's involved in a sales scam where he checks out home security and the gang he's in robs the right places. He doesn't care about hurting people but is angry at being bossed around by the leader. He wants to be rich and respected and takes risks to prove his worth to the gang.*

The things that could go wrong:

○ *Mickey's arrested by the police and forced to inform on his gang.*

○ *He's beaten up by a homeowner who's been robbed and wants revenge.*

○ *He's set up by the leader to take the blame for a break-in that went wrong.*

○ *The leader spreads lies about him and humiliates him in front of the gang.*

○ *He's excluded from the gang after beating up the leader.*

○ *He sets up a daredevil stunt to impress the gang but hurts himself badly.*

○ *He realises the gang wants to rob his sister's house and refuses to do it.*

o *He loses everything after someone breaks into his place and robs it.*

o *The leader's wife falls in love with him and wants to have an affair.*

o *Mickey falls in love with the leader.*

➢ Number the above complications from one to nine where 'one' isn't so bad and 'nine' is absolutely terrible. Put them in order from one to nine.

➢ Now pick the five you feel connect into a possible narrative and write them out. Create clear rising action where the central problem continually gets worse. Finally, create one more problem for the end, making it the worst you can possibly think of.

➢ Now pick a problem or situation from one of your stories. Brainstorm ten possible obstacles to the character's want. Put them in order, smallest first and biggest at the end. Where are you missing steps? What new obstacles could fill those gaps, to get a smooth rising action from one step to another? Is there cause and effect in how the obstacles connect? Is there natural movement and a rising order?

Making things worse

Traditionally, Act Two contains a series of setbacks that get progressively worse. This usually culminates in a low point at the end of the act where the character literally or metaphorically hits rock bottom. Because Act Two houses the bulk of the drama and momentum needs to be sustained, it can often be the hardest part to write. Stories can easily become repetitive, and character development lost in the telling.

To develop skills in plotting, it's a good idea to map out a series of obstacles that your protagonist may encounter on their journey before you begin to write the actual script. You may have done this at treatment stage, but it's always useful to think specifically about the beats and how to make things progressively worse for your character.

> *Petra's a high-school teacher who's losing her marbles. She was once brilliant, loved by her students, but since her husband died, has lost control both of her classes and her life. The story hits rock bottom when Petra finally flips and holds her class hostage.*

> Write a series of beats for Petra's demise, starting at point A, returning after the summer holidays in which her husband died, and ending at point B, where she takes her class hostage. Write as many beats as you can, thinking about what would push Petra further and further on a downward spiral. Try to write at least thirty beats.

> Now go back to the list and pick out fifteen beats that you think offer the most dramatic potential, or most originality, to sustain a good Act Two. Look at the order and move the beats around so they create the steepest decline for Petra and the most engaging journey for the audience. Keep rearranging and tweaking the beats until you're happy they provide the best fit.

> Finally, look at the fifteen beats and consider whether each has an emotional as well as a physical quality. Is there a strong enough sense of Petra's inner character arc alongside the pure plot? Where there are emotional gaps, play around with the beats to see what their emotional qualities could be.

Plants and payoffs

There's something really rewarding about plants and payoffs in screenplays. Audiences like to be given clues for which they then anticipate a resolution, or to be given a payoff from which they can backtrack to find the plants that were seeded into the plot. You could say that a screenplay is one big plant and payoff: a question is set or a problem posed, which is then answered or resolved.

Specific plants and payoffs, though, work on a micro-level. A plant here is a dramatic element that's seeded-in somewhere in the early stages of the screenplay and then replayed or referred to several more times as the story develops. Then, towards the end, it finds a natural and meaningful resolution; the plant is 'paid off.' Plants and payoffs can come in many forms depending on the story and genre, but are often found as words or expressions (repeated, rephrased, twisted), objects (passed on, built, destroyed), or even minor characters (reappearing).

> Take the following situation, which could be the start to a screenplay:

> *Liz has been for an interview at her workplace, hoping that she'll be given promotion to team leader. Her nemesis, Alan, has also been interviewed for the same position. They're both working at their*

*desks when manager Sasha comes over and tells them that Alan
has been successful. Alan gloats, pulling a pre-bought cake out of
his drawer to celebrate. As he lights an also pre-bought sparkler, he
smirks at Liz and tells her, 'All's fair in love and war.'*

➤ From this scenario, choose three elements that could be considered
plants. Think about the detail and work out how it could be developed
further as the story progresses.

➤ With each plant, think of five possible payoffs. Think carefully about
the type of story that this set-up could develop into, and choose the
payoffs accordingly.

➤ When you have five payoffs for each, plot out three specific occasions
where the plant could reappear in the story before the payoff. Think
carefully about why it would be used again at each specific moment,
and how it would develop or change each time.

Tying-up loose ends

The purpose of structure is to orchestrate a set of responses in the
audience, and nowhere is this more evident than at the end. It's the
culmination of all that's happened so far and all that will happen after
the story's ended (where the characters will go next and how the audience will respond). Structurally, then, it's the climax of all the drama
that we've seen as well as the incitement of what will be felt when the
credits roll. It's the point where both character and audience reflect on
what's happened and find emotional resolution, and it isn't uncommon
for themes and character journeys to be reiterated at the end of a screenplay to clarify this sense of closure.

➤ Think about a film you know well, and write down what you think it
gives its audience. Consider characters, situations, locations/worlds,
central dramatic and thematic questions, feelings, emotions and
themes. Try to pinpoint a strong sense of what the film's about, and
how it communicates this.

➤ Now watch the final fifteen or so minutes and think about how the
screenwriter has brought all these ideas out and tied them up. Even
if it's a film with an ambiguous ending, think how this relates to its

theme or style or message. Specific questions you might want to ask of the ending are:

o Which characters do we see, and why?

o Which locations are used?

o What do people say to each other?

o How does the pace reflect the intended feelings of the audience?

o Are situations that have already been seen re-enacted?

o Are lines of dialogue or expressions already used repeated?

o What's the final image?

➢ When you've done this, look at the ending of your screenplays and ask yourself the same questions. Do the answers match with what you want the audience to feel? Is there further work to be done on the structure to ensure a more powerful ending?

7 Reimagining structure

Understanding classical structure as an essential building block in the screenwriter's craft goes hand-in-hand with this chapter on examining further ways of working with story architecture. They're not opposing ways of working, but rather an extension of thinking about deep structure as a way of expressing a story's themes and purpose.

This chapter explores different frameworks of composition beyond that of the classical single protagonist, three-act narrative. The exercises that follow are useful when probing a script's potential structure, even if it's only playing around with possibilities. They're also useful when first thinking about ideas, to see if there are any new and interesting ways of telling a story that might not usually be considered.

Working your way through these exercises should give you a deeper understanding of the role of structure in screenwriting, and its inherent creative opportunities. This means that, as a writer, you'll be prepared to be more open and innovative with ideas when they arise, and will be able to find effective ways of working with narrative that really serve the needs of the story.

Alternative routes

The essential point about structure is that it's the relationship of different moments to each other within the whole that creates significance and meaning. Whether you consciously intend to write in chronological form or not, it's indispensible to experiment with the order of events during rewriting, to ensure you arrive at the best storytelling pattern.

A story may feel like it has a natural order and no other way it can be told. This is never the case. There are many films that follow a somewhat non-linear surface plot even though it's not flagged up as a selling feature. They contain particular moments where scenes are shifted around to create a better sequence by which to reveal the story.

Working with story steps on index cards is a large part of the rewriting process for many writers as it gives a clear overview of story architecture. To experiment with how structure can help enhance a story – not for its own sake, but when it's relevant – try this exercise.

➢ Study the following plot points and the story they formulate:

   o *Aatu and Pekka hunt whales in the North Sea.*

   o *During the struggle to catch the whale, Aatu falls in the water.*

   o *Aatu has a mystical experience as the whale saves him from drowning.*

   o *Back on board, Aatu refuses to let Pekka continue the hunt.*

   o *Pekka accidentally kills Aatu in a fight, but the whale gets away.*

   o *On land, Pekka claims Aatu drowned in an accident. Consumed by guilt, Pekka stops fishing and starts to drink.*

   o *The spirit of Aatu visits Pekka and shows him how to make amends. Pekka starts a whale-watching company, teaching people about the beauty of whales.*

➢ Write each of the above plot points on a separate index card. Spread the cards out, mixing them up so they're no longer in linear sequence. Pick a card and experiment with what plot points could come before or after it. Create new combinations and test them out. You can also do this randomly, placing scenes together without thinking, to see what happens. It's important to allow plenty of time for this and not to make assumptions about what will work.

➢ Find at least two new ways to tell this story by changing the order of the scenes. Write out the new structure. What happens to the story? How will the audience experience it? Does tone, theme or genre change? Which do you like best and why?

➤ You might find a totally new narrative shape or you might keep a mainly linear structure, but spot places where scenes can be swapped around to create more drama and resonance. Whether you make large or small changes, many or few, this exercise deepens understanding of individual story sections and the bigger picture.

➤ Try this with your own script. Locate five to fifteen essential plot points and play with the order, seeing how creating new relationships between story steps shifts meaning and changes the audience's emotional experience.

Where are you going?

A screenplay can have a surface structure where the external order of events seems non-linear, but where the internal, emotional journey follows a classical structure of progression, moving from want to need. When writing a non-linear script, carefully examining both the action (plot) structure and the emotional (arc) structure lets you see how they relate and form the story. It's often scripts with clear character progression that resonate with audiences, whatever the surface structure.

➤ Read the following non-linear plot events, and locate an emotional beat in each. Also define what changes occur in or between them, either outside or inside the character.

Premise: *Rowena is mourning the death of her husband and can't get over it.*

Order of plot events:

1 *Rowena sits alone in a silent room, staring at a bottle of sleeping pills.*

2 *Rowena and Anthony argue. Anthony runs out, slamming the door.*

3 *Rowena walks along windswept cliffs. She looks down at the swirling sea.*

4 *Furious, Anthony drives too fast along a country road.*

5 *Rowena stands perfectly still by a large tree with a heavy broken branch.*

6 *Rowena's friend Jay calls and leaves a message, asking if they can meet.*

7 *Rowena ignores the phone and searches the attic for old love letters.*

8 *As Rowena reads, she hears a trapped bird. After a long, upsetting struggle, she finally releases it out of the window. As it flies away, she starts crying.*

9 *Anthony sits in the car. Cracked windshield, blood everywhere. He watches a bird sing in the tree, a peaceful look on his face.*

10 *Rowena wakes early the next morning, listening to birdsong outside the window.*

11 *She gets up and goes swimming naked in the cold bracing sea.*

12 *Rowena and Jay have coffee together. Jay invites her to join a music appreciation club and Rowena accepts, saying she thinks she'd like that very much.*

➤ When locating the inner emotional beats of the plot events, ask yourself what Rowena feels in each. Who is she, what does she do? Does she takes any decisions, does she act or react?

➤ Analyse the resulting character arc to see how it progresses. Even though the physical events are jumbled up in time, is Rowena's own emotional development through the story linear? How close or far away is she to her want and need? Is there a change within Rowena in coming to terms with grief, death and life? How does the audience follow her struggle? What is Rowena's emotional journey, and what is the audience's journey?

➤ Now you have the skeleton of the linear emotional journey, examine the structure of the surface plot. What's gained by telling this story in a non-chronological way? How does it create a felt experience of the character's situation, both her want and need? What tensions or expectations are created from the order of events? What shape does the story have and how does it relate to its theme? What do you learn about the relationship between inner and outer story, and how to work creatively with non-linear structure?

Multiple protagonists

The key principle of multiple protagonist stories is that the protagonists each have their own emotional arc, but by and large share the physical journey and, crucially, are brought together by the same inciting incident. This allows a screenwriter to explore a variety of responses that may occur from one catalytic event, and is an effective way of showing how we as a society react to shared events with different emotional nuances.

➢ Take the following scenario as the basis for a multiple protagonist story:

> *Katy is about to give birth to her first baby. Her husband Josh has taken a few weeks off work to be there for the birth. Katy's mum and dad, Maureen and Alf, have come over from their retirement property in Spain, and Katy's brother, Hugo, has come over from Australia, where he now lives.*

➢ For each character, list five things that being back in the family fold might bring up. What potential issues might arise? What might each character have to confront?

➢ Now take one issue from each character (as per your lists) and put them together, creating five potential issues in total. Starting with the arrival of everyone at Katy's house, map out five character arcs that might take place over the course of the stay. Try to keep the family together as much as possible, using each character to bring out another's arc.

➢ How easy or difficult was this? Did organic journeys arise, or did you have to tweak the character arcs to fit the situation? How much did you think about the characters' backstory to create a compelling multiple protagonist narrative? Did one central theme hold all the stories together?

➢ Try this exercise again, this time choosing five other issues from the character lists. What kinds of stories emerge this time? How effective do you think the inciting incident is in bringing together and teasing out these stories? What other inciting incidents might be useful for this family's story?

Parallel stories

Screenplays using the parallel narrative structure model are similar to multiple protagonist stories, but differ in that they often aim to explore a common theme or emotion through different character perspectives. From experiencing a set of interwoven stories, some of which might take place in different worlds and eras, the audience is invited to connect them through a consideration of the thematic or emotional driver.

The key to parallel storytelling is to find interesting, original and complementary characters through whom a universal theme or emotion can be explored. As usual, the core of the screenplay lies in theme or emotion, but its unique texture is found in its structural execution: an idea told through juxtaposing parallel characters and worlds.

➢ Take the theme of *abandonment* and create five diverse protagonists to explore it. Start by asking:

  o What does abandonment mean to you?

  o What could it mean to others?

  o What different ways can you be abandoned?

  o Would abandonment have different significance in different cultures?

  o How might locations or worlds suggest a different sense of abandonment?

  o Where might you expect abandonment?

  o Where might you not expect it?

  o Have you ever felt abandoned?

➢ With your five protagonists, sketch out their individual plots using broad brushstrokes. Think about both their physical and emotional journeys, and what their individual arc is saying about the common theme.

➢ When you've done this, think horizontally across the protagonists' stories and see if you can find points at which their stories interweave. What order might they take? Would you spend time with them in equal measures? How might you express the theme most potently through character and plot juxtapositions? Are there ways in which the individual stories don't have to be told linearly when they co-exist in this structural format?

Mix it up

A film always has a beginning, middle and end; but the beginning, middle and end that the audience experiences isn't always the same as that which the characters experience. The order of events as they happen to characters is always chronological (unless it's a time-travel story), but the telling of those events to an audience might be offered in any sequence.

In this way, an awareness gap is created between audience and character. Through this gap, the writer can play with expectations and use structure to create tension, rhythm, subtext and drama. A simple way to explore your story further to see how it can be most effectively told is to swap beginnings and endings and see what happens.

➢ Read the following premise:

> Jake's a war correspondent who meets enigmatic artist Kathy. As they fall in love, she reveals she has insider contacts in the underground movement. In their quest for truth, they go deep into political subterfuge and intrigue, only to discover the imminent revolution is a cover-up controlled by the government. They flee for their lives, ending up with false identities in a small town. They start making art based on their experiences and create their own cultural revolution.

➢ Find at least five different beginning, middle and end points for this story. For instance, begin it at the end, then in the middle; end it at the beginning, then the middle; start at the end, end with the beginning. How does each story structure shape and affect the audience experience?

➢ Now look at this premise again, but this time through the lens of these two themes:

1 *What is the value of truth?*

2 *How far will you corrupt yourself to achieve legitimate ends?*

➢ Which beginning and end would best serve each separate theme? How could structure create mystery, intrigue, doubt and resolution to highlight different meanings? Experiment with perspectives and timelines. How else could the order of events be mixed up to make the audience experience potent and relevant? Try making the story circular instead of linear, so that it ends where it began. What theme will this emphasise? How does the audience's understanding of the situation change? What theme emerges from your version of this story?

Flashing back

The main purpose of a flashback is to illuminate what happened in the past and how and why this affects the present. Films and TV dramas using flashback in an innovative structural manner can have great sophistication, playing with the audience's mind and asking them to actively construct meaning. The danger with the flashback is that it becomes a gimmick and, instead of adding to, detracts from the story. Flashbacks can also have a tendency to interrupt the dramatic drive of a story, as the writer feels compelled to convey past information to the audience. If not done well, this can make a script static, clunky and slow.

➤ Imagine a film that opens like this:

> *An almighty row between boyfriend and girlfriend Giuseppe and Rosa. They're chasing each other round their villa and verbally abusing each other. Things begin to get physical and Giuseppe becomes more violent. Rosa tries to escape but Giuseppe runs after her and as they get to the top of the stairs and tussle, she accidentally pushes him. He falls down the stairs and is killed instantly. Rosa slowly descends the stairs and, seeing a pool of blood around Giuseppe's head, whispers to herself, 'Why didn't I just tell you?'*

This hook provides not only dramatic tension, but also intrigue. We want to know why they're fighting, and what it was she didn't tell him.

➤ Come up with three different stories that could be told in flashback, starting with the sequence above. Vary the stories as much as you can, thinking about different motivations for the row. Work through each idea and brainstorm how they might be best told through flashback. Think about the type of flashback structure each might benefit from, and the positioning of the flashbacks throughout the narrative. You might want to consider:

o Does the story need lots or a little flashback?

o How integral to the present story is the past?

o Should a flashback just be used to show the trigger for the story, or should the whole story be told in the past?

o Should the flashback be continuous or fragmented?

○ Could there be any images or scenes that are repeated in flashback?

○ How many times should we flashback?

○ Through whose perspective should the flashback be seen?

○ How do you want the audience to engage with the flashback?

➢ Finally, think how the story in the present might end. Depending on the approach to flashback that you've taken, what would be the most appropriate ending? What has the flashback told us about Giuseppe and Rosa, and how do we want their story to be resolved?

Telling the time

There's an intimate relationship between story structure and time. Linear storytelling unfolds events in chronological order. Other narratives shift sequences around to jumble up time, while yet others create parallel timelines that connect through plot, world or theme.

By working with time as structure, the writer creates a new relationship between events, people and outcomes. A different feeling of cause and effect is forged, as elements influence each other thematically, if not physically. Sometimes characters are aware of each other, sometimes they're not, but narratively they have a relationship to each other through the different timelines. This way, the writer can create sophisticated story experiences where the structure reveals a bigger picture of how things fit together and affect each other.

Timelines don't only refer to flashbacks and backstory. Working with time as a narrative element means it can appear as repetitive time, circular time, parallel time, regressive time, or fragmented time. Each creates its own structural shape. Usually it's best to find a temporal form that naturally fits with story and theme rather than inventing one for the novelty of it.

➢ Read these two separate storylines, played out in different time periods:

> *Indira is a biologist working on a research project studying the probable extinction of a butterfly species. She's good at her job, on her way to the top. But somehow she feels as if she's missing something, though she can't put her finger on it. She needs to present concrete research findings before the funding runs out.*

> *As the only niece of a Victorian industry magnate, Samantha lives a life of leisure. To give herself something to do, she starts her own private butterfly farm. Initially she does this to collect and catalogue every species, but eventually it's for the sheer joy it gives her. Her unique approach brings her a deep and extensive understanding of butterflies.*

➢ Brainstorm at least five ways these two stories could connect. How might their paths cross, literally, thematically or symbolically? What moments need to be shown? How can the two inform one another? How can the characters help or hinder one another, if not literally then through what they mean to each other? At what points should they meet or affect each other? What information does the audience need about one to understand and engage with the other?

➢ Draw a curve for both timelines, showing their narrative shapes as separate stories. Compare the shapes of the curves. Do they share any specific turning points? Is one up when the other is down? How can cause and effect work between them, so that a thematic relationship is established for the audience, even if the characters are not aware of it?

➢ Write a story where the two timelines combine and create a whole. It should include both characters playing major parts, not just one reading about the other. Finally, write another version where you combine these stories with a third, new timeline. What do you learn about storytelling by using a parallel timeframe?

When working with timelines, always write out each story as its own separate arc. This will give you a clear idea of the independent strands, allowing you to see the best way to connect and harmonise them.

Shapeshifting

Because it's not such a rigid form, a non-linear story is an opportunity to work extensively with the concept of *deep structure* – a kind of structural subext. Deep structure refers to the hidden shape of the narrative. It's a cinematic subconscious that orchestrates the audience's emotional experience through the story. In this way, screenplay structure is akin to music, touching people on a deep level through its form, not only its content. Working architecturally with deep structure allows storytelling to become subtle, sophisticated and powerful. It's a skill well worth developing, as it can also enhance classical screenplay form. To practise working with it, writers should consider which narrative shape can best subconsciously express their theme, resulting in a fitting emotional experience for the audience.

➤ Consider the following themes:

   ○ *We're all pawns in the game of life.*

   ○ *Magic's in the small things, if only you remember to look.*

   ○ *The past will haunt you until you solve its secret.*

➤ In turn, free-associate words, feelings and shapes that each theme makes you think of.

➤ Brainstorm five possible stories that could express each of the themes. What narrative shape would you use? Consider all the techniques covered in this chapter: timelines, character perspectives, mixing up order of events, comparing surface structure with emotional structure, working with multiple protagonists, flashbacks and parallel stories. Don't forget to work with tempo and rhythm, creating space for pauses and reflection. How do you feel the deep structure will affect the audience experience?

➤ Choose a script you're working on and uncover its deep structure, then think further about how this shape could relate better to the overall theme.

8 Defining beginnings and endings

Though beginnings and endings might seem relatively short sections within a screenplay, it's crucial to get them right. The beginning is the door that opens and invites the audience into the story, and carries the responsibility of setting the tone and asking the right dramatic questions. The ending is the final note that the audience carry with them as they drift away from the closing credits, and determines how they'll remember and relate to the whole story. As such, they're both worth close examination to ensure that they serve the script as well as possible. During rewrite stages, it's an excellent idea to work closely on beginnings and endings, not only to get them right but to see what further understanding of the story they might bring.

When revisiting the beginning and the ending, the writer has to look closely at what question the story is really asking, and what answer it is providing. Through close scrutiny, the writer needs to work out whether they're the right questions for the story, or whether there's still more work to do. Beginnings and endings are complicated dramatic entities: as well as addressing the core dramatic questions, they also need to introduce and resolve characters, world and theme, establish the rules and internal logic of the world, and fulfil a contract between the drama and its audience.

Starting over

In screenwriting, the beginning isn't always the right place to start. A script has two different sequential narratives: the chronological order of events as they happen, and the order in which they're told. Choosing the right start is about setting the right dramatic context for the audience. The opening moment may be a scene totally unrelated to early events. Many scripts also start too soon; they begin in the backstory and trace out all the steps, instead of jumping in where the story takes off. Instead of assuming a particular entry point as the obvious beginning, exploring alternatives can make a script more engaging, intriguing and dynamic.

➤ Take a script or story you're working on. Find at least five moments in the current first half that could be potential beginnings. Try each and see what happens to the story. What makes it most dynamic, intriguing, fitting to form and genre? What seems the latest possible moment to start it?

➤ Take the same story and write out, in a sentence each, the following:

  ○ Inciting incident.

  ○ End of Act One (or first major turning point).

  ○ Mid point (or next big turning point).

  ○ End of Act Two (or turning point in last half).

  ○ Resolution.

➤ One at a time, try these out as the beginning of your script. What happens? What expectations are set up? What questions are raised? What dramatic tension is created? How does each beginning relate to theme and inner character journey? Does it suggest a new structure? How should it end, if it begins in this way?

Setting the dramatic question

The opening of a screenplay is designed to create intrigue about a character's life and situation, posing a series of questions about them that will be explored through the rest of the story. Ultimately, all these questions feed into both the central dramatic question (CDQ) and the central thematic question (CTQ) of the screenplay. The opening is, therefore, important in generating audience interest and setting audience expectations.

➢ Take as a premise the CDQ: *Will Luther brainwash the clan before it's too late?* and the CTQ: *Will Luther learn the importance of friendship, or not?* Brainstorm five ways that this screenplay could open. Think in terms of a sequence, where you build a sense of the CDQ and the CTQ through a compilation of scenes. Aim to sketch out about ten minutes of screenplay. Think creatively about styles, worlds and characters, remembering that your aim is to articulate both the CDQ and the CTQ.

➢ Now reverse the exercise. Look at each of your five sequence ideas and come up with five other possible CDQs and CTQs for each. What might the sequences suggest other than that specified here? Do your ideas contain other possible CDQs and CTQs? Could the scenes have more than one meaning? Could there be a 'twist', where you suggest one thing but then reveal something else? What do you learn about the relationship between opening sequences and the core dramatic and thematic questions?

Image is everything

It's useful to consider how an opening image can be used to symbolise the story ahead. Whether the image is part of the first scene or whether it's more abstract and sits outside the story, like a prologue, it can carry important meaning relating to the screenplay's themes or emotions, the protagonist's journey, or the story's perspective. It can also set the tone and serves as the audience's very first connection to the story.

➢ With each of the following premises, brainstorm ten images that could kick-start the screenplay. Try to use both actual scene starts and abstract 'prologue' images, and think carefully about themes and emotions, tone, character journeys and perspectives.

    ○ *A short film following the life of Terry, a sixty-year-old milkman struggling to compete with the big supermarkets.*

    ○ *A feature film about a group of teenage friends who go on holiday to Greece. They're all about to leave home in various ways, and see the holiday as a final blowout before they move into their adult lives.*

- *A TV series set in a crime-ridden suburb of a major city. The series follows a group of corrupt police officers who'll go to any lengths to save the name of the city.*

- *A short film set in a park, dealing with themes of nature and beauty. The film captures a day in the life of the park.*

First impressions

If a story consists mainly of one character's journey, the beginning needs to consider how to introduce them to the audience. How they first meet them will have bearing on how interested they become in their story. It's not always necessary to present a character as likeable or logical, or to reveal everything about them up front. First impressions are about creating impact, and can be achieved in a number of ways to intrigue and surprise the audience. It needs to work both on a scene level (dramatic entrance) and on a story level (fitting character arc and theme). It's important to know how the audience should think about the character when they first see them, and how this impression should change during the story.

➤ Read the premise below and write three different scenes showing possible first moments of meeting Filippa.

> *Filippa is fifteen and wants to leave home. She hates her alcoholic mother, hates herself and feels lost. She's unsure of what life has to offer and dreams of finding someone who can tell her what it's all about. She hitchhikes to the city and is given a crash course in life. Exploited and discarded, she's forced to find her own way and become her own strength. She survives – but with scars both inside and out.*

➤ Each first impression scene should be no longer than half a page. Think about how Filippa enters. Where in the world is she? What's she doing? How is she behaving? What do you want the audience to feel and know about her? What do you want them to question? Create different versions in which Filippa will arouse less or more sympathy, interest and trust.

Pain and problems

Part of creating a beginning is establishing the problem of the story – the pain that will cause a character or world to react and change. If you're unsure where to start, a good option is to look for a moment of suffering or difficulty. If you begin right in the middle of this, it plunges the audience headlong into the story without time to think. It may not be right for all scripts, but it's always worth trying as it creates drama, intrigue and a strong tempo. This is particularly helpful when the main character is complex and may not be immediately likeable, since putting them in peril or pain creates a degree of sympathy, and the audience is more likely to become interested in their fate.

➢ Read the premise below and write three opening scenes that show Bula in pain. Then write three opening scenes that show Bula's problem. Experiment with widely different approaches, trying to think beyond the obvious.

> *Bula the beaver has been captured and trained to perform at a tourist attraction. She's aggressive and unreliable, with a nasty reputation. She'll become the heroine of the story as she tries to escape and find her way back to the wild.*

➢ Look at your various opening scenes and think about what feelings they might arouse in an audience. Would they feel sympathy with Bula? How might they become interested in her situation? Are there doubts and uncertainties in the scene that could help fuel the story while ensuring that the audience stays engaged?

Essential facts

Opening sequences often have to impart a great deal of information so that the audience can understand what's going on. This exposition can weigh down the story, making it slow and dull. Though some exposition is necessary, it doesn't all have to be given upfront. Instead, it can be offered at later relevant dramatic moments to create interest and surprise. A beginning is not only about providing answers but also about creating questions, so it's important that there's a balance between information and intrigue.

➢ Choose a film or TV series episode and watch the first fifteen minutes. Write down all the essential facts you learn. Watch the scenes again and analyse how the information is given. How is it made to feel engaging? What questions does it set up? What's the balance and rhythm between information and action?

➢ Now look at the first fifteen mins of your own script. If possible, work with a partner, swapping scripts and reading through each other's. Highlight the information given and write it out as a list of facts. Think about what you really need to understand. What do you need to know now? What can you know later to help create suspense and dramatic tension? When is the right dramatic moment to reveal each piece of information?

➢ Feed back to your partner about what you found, and listen to them give feedback to you. You can also do this exercise on your own script, but if you do, be objective when highlighting the facts rather than writing what you think you're showing.

Opening with voiceover

Scripts that use voiceover narration need to pay particular attention to the beginning since it creates an immediate bond between audience and character. And not only that: the voice also has to connect with an audience in such a way that an immediate impression of the story's perspective is offered. As with an opening image, opening with voiceover can set the tone of the story, quickly allude to themes and emotions, allow us to understand how an unfamiliar world works, and even act as a 'plant' to be paid off later. Although voiceover can be tricky to get right and can sometimes seem like an easy way out, it's very effective in setting dramatic focus and clearly positioning the audience in the narrative.

➢ Rewrite the following bland voiceover monologue according to each of the situations then given. Vary style, tone and pace as much as feels appropriate, and change words and expressions where you think this will be useful.

'It wasn't always like this. We used to be happy, once upon a time. When we met, it was like there was electricity between us all the time. We were each other's charge. The days out . . . the nights in . . . how I miss what we had. It's hard to pinpoint exactly when it all changed, but I'm certain it had something to do with him. When he arrived on the scene, we just . . . Well, it's now or never.'

○ *Peter knows that his wife's having an affair, but hasn't confronted her about it yet. He's just found out that he's dying of cancer, and so isn't sure whether to tell her or not. He wonders whether just to pack up and leave while she's at work.*

○ *Peter's getting frustrated that his wife isn't spending much time with him any more now they've had their first child. He knows that he shouldn't be jealous of his own son, but can't help feeling this way. He's scared he'll be pushed further and further away.*

○ *Peter's deeply suspicious of his wife's long-lost brother, who turned up a few months ago and is still living with them. He's getting paranoid and jealous, thinking the brother has some nasty trick up his sleeve.*

➤ Did the voiceover change as much as you'd imagined, or more than you'd expected? How many times did you go over it and play around with the structure as well as the words? Do you feel it puts the audience in a clear position about Peter's situation? Does it make things too clear? What specific changes did you make to fit the stories' perspectives? If you have the chance, get someone to read them aloud so you can really listen and assess their impact.

Full stop

The ending is the point where you leave the audience – the full stop to your story. You hand over, and the audience goes away with emotional resonance: thoughts, memories, feelings, questions. However good a script has been up to this point, if the end is a disappointment the audience will feel let down. The end may only be one element in the story, but it can effect the meaning of the whole thing.

Sometimes writers are so happy to get to the end and feel finished that they rush the last third of the screenplay. Instead, make the most of your ending. This is what the whole story has been building up to, so let the audience (and characters) enjoy it. Give the ending the room it deserves.

But how do you know when you've come to the end, and that it's right and fitting? One way is to see the end as the answer to the dramatic questions asked in the beginning. If you know what the question was, it should be relatively easy to work out the answer. However, it's important to remember both CDQ and CTQ. Sometimes writers finish off the plot but forget to wrap up the thematic resolution. A good ending will consider both.

➢ If the CDQ is *Will Diego escape from the violent mafia gang?* and the CTQ is *Will Diego leave his old life behind and find a new way of being?*, possible dramatic resolutions are:

  ○ Yes he escapes.

  ○ No he doesn't.

  ○ It's not certain.

➢ Possible thematic resolutions will be related to how much he's left his old life behind; if it'll still haunt him; what he's left with; if there's a new way of being. Also consider whether this will be clearly stated or merely hinted at.

➢ Create three possible dramatic resolutions and three thematic resolutions to the following story. Write them out with as much specific detail as you can:

  ○ CDQ: *Will Naz manage to make a living as a chef and make his family proud?*

  ○ CTQ: *Are the sacrifices greater than the rewards when you live your life for others?*

➢ Now mix different dramatic resolutions with different thematic resolutions. Which combinations do you like and why? How do the different endings affect story and theme? How do they provide meaning and resonance?

Approaching endings in this systematic way gives the story cohesion and resonance. It provides clarity which can then be shaded with subtlety.

Last dance

One of the most rewarding ways to check if your story is functioning well is to try a number of different endings. Even if you're sure your current ending is right, such experimentation can help to clarify theme and character arcs, and bring deeper meaning. Taking radical steps can create extra sparkle, and daring to look at something you've avoided helps release new ideas and energy. Even if you still choose your original ending, you'll be clearer and more confident about why it's right.

➢ Choose a story that already has an ending, either your own or an existing screenplay. Invent the following new endings:

- The protagonist gets exactly what they want.

- The protagonist doesn't get what they want.

- The protagonist fails and the antagonist wins.

- The protagonist dies at the end (think of different ways this could happen and the many effects it could have, including positive ones).

- The protagonist ends up back where they started, either physically, emotionally or both.

➢ Write each more than once to find a range of outlandish and credible ideas. Compare them to see differences and similarities. What do you like? What do you learn from each? How could each help the story, either at the end or beforehand?

Mirror, mirror

Beginnings and endings sometimes present the same event or situation to highlight what's changed during the story. Whether it's a repeated situation, character or perspective, it's usually done to reinforce the story arc – the whole point of the journey the audience has shared. The use of mirror scenes can capture both physical and emotional change, and create great audience satisfaction and understanding. By using mirror scenes, meaning often becomes clear and doesn't have to be spelled out in obvious ways.

➢ Create five mirror scenes or sequences for the following story arcs. Think in as much detail as possible, considering elements such as location, mood, dialogue, and visuals.

○ *A group of ducks pull together against all the odds to save their beloved lake. They learn the value of teamwork and standing up for one's rights.*

○ *A promising football star is led into a world of deceit and corruption, resulting in him being banned from the game for life.*

○ *An investment banker learns the true value of humanity when he's made redundant and re-trains as a mathematics teacher.*

○ *A strict mother reconsiders her religious beliefs after her daughter comes out as a lesbian.*

One step beyond

What can be really wonderful about endings is that they give the audience exactly what they long for: resolution, satisfaction, a sense of completion. But they can also feel too obvious, so it's important to consider giving the audience what they want in a way they don't expect. There's nothing wrong with simple endings if they're right; but sometimes it's useful to lift the lid and see what else is in the box, to take the story a step further. This is how false endings and twists work, where the writer pretends to end the story then releases one last thunderbolt.

Such an added twist can make a script exciting and memorable. However, if the twist is created merely to shock, it's nearly always a bad idea. Like all endings, a twist needs to support the story and help the pieces fall into place. There's no point stunning the audience for the sake of it, if it doesn't fit with story and theme. There has to be sense and symmetry in the twist, not just surprise. The point is to make the story resonate deeper with the audience, not to make the writer feel clever, and definitely not to cheat the audience. A twist can't carry the story, as it comes right at the end – the story has to make sense long before the twist. Such endings are complicated, but can give a lot of added value if done well.

➢ Look at an ending to one of your stories and brainstorm five ways it could go one step beyond what's currently there. For instance, if the current ending is *Kofi and Kwame make up and accept each other as blood brothers*, a final twist could be:

○ *They discover they didn't have the same biological father after all, but nevertheless feel like brothers.*

○ *Kwame is now forced to kill his brother because of an age-old pact.*

○ *Kofi reveals he's lived under a false identity and asks Kwame to forgive him.*

Note that these are not about replacing the expected end, but delivering it and then adding something extra on top. A good ending isn't to do with what's most exciting, original or surprising, but with what's most fitting for the story, theme and character.

Damp squib

A good script can be completely spoiled by a bad ending. It can make an audience feel cheated, by setting up expectations that aren't satisfied or getting out of a problem too easily. If the contract between story and audience isn't honoured, the whole screenplay can collapse like a house of cards. A good ending shows that the writer knows what the story's about and why they want to tell it.

By the time you come round to the end, the characters are in big trouble and the audience can't imagine how they'll get out of it. It's a challenge, but also part of the delight of devising an ending, and the writer's responsibility is to solve this problem in a fitting, exciting and dramatically relevant way.

Endings are also tricky because they only offer limited alternatives: happy, sad, or open. The writer has to fulfill the obligations of the story but the available options can make it feel too simplistic. If writers are afraid of being obvious, sentimental or boring, there's a danger of over-compensating and making endings too obscure or complicated.

It's important that writers allow themselves to test many endings, even those that seem terrible. If you let seemingly awful endings out into the light, they no longer hang around and haunt the script. They won't block the writing process and might even bestow a gem or two. To get a sense of what kind of endings satisfy you, try the following then apply it to your own stories.

➢ Using Filippa's premise from 'First Impressions' (p. 95), write five possible, truly terrible endings. Make them bad in different ways: obvious, sentimental, not honouring the story, etc. Dare to go where you'd never normally tread. What happens?

➢ Put them in order of the worst first. Why are they bad? What exactly is it that feels dissatisfying? Is there anything you feel interested in that could work? How could you use this detail in a better ending?

➢ How does it feel to be allowed to write such endings?

9 Weaving worlds

Finding the right world is a major part of creating a good story. The world itself may not be the most essential aspect, but as a container that makes the story possible and sustains it in the right way, it's vitally important. A well-chosen world can create a specific audience experience; a particular tone and feeling that the plot cannot convey on its own. A world also has its own innate dramatic potential, and your choice can both help and hinder how the story's told.

A world can belong to a particular character, and imposing a new world on the character creates challenges that they have to work with. This may not be part of the plot per se, but helps to fuel it.

A well-chosen world can bring a familiar story alive and make it feel fresh and inspiring. Many successful screenplays take a classic storyline (*Romeo and Juliet*, *The Ugly Duckling*, *Beauty and the Beast*) and set it in an unusual environment. This makes the script feel new and exciting, giving it relevance for a contemporary audience. Dramatic milieu is something writers should not take for granted; digging deeper to find a world you hadn't thought of can be like striking gold. This is especially true for TV series, where finding the right world is a decisive factor in whether the project will survive or not.

Worlds aren't just important at the macro level, they're also effective at the micro level. Careful consideration of location when writing scenes can create added drama and power. You'll find an exercise about scene worlds here, and more in Chapter 12.

Reframing the familiar

There are numerous examples of familiar stories set in unfamiliar worlds that make them seem fresh, exciting and relevant. Writers often take the concept of worlds for granted, using the most obvious or the first idea that comes to them without considering how it can be actively worked up. The idea of worlds can be a great starting point for a story, and if carefully considered, an excellent way to increase the sales potential of an idea.

➢ Take the basic Cinderella story premise:

> *A young girl gets a new stepfamily that treats her badly. She dreams of better things – that someone will come and take her away to a place where she'll be appreciated. She meets a helper who gives her the ability and confidence to secretly go with her stepsisters to a big party, but has to leave early to make sure no one discovers her real identity. Her dreams come true when the prince falls in love with her and comes to find her.*

➢ Consider the various worlds in the traditional version of this story, and what their functions are. How do the worlds mirror Cinderella's current situation and her dreams? How do the worlds bring in different characters? Which worlds have thematic relevance?

➢ Now brainstorm at least twenty different worlds that this story could also take place in. Think not only about geography, but also about lifestyle and era. Disregard nothing, however silly or improbable it may seem. Compile the worlds into a list.

➢ Now choose your five favourite worlds. Try out the basic storyline in each world and brainstorm notes to yourself about how it works or not. What happens? What changes? What ideas do you get? How could it evolve in interesting ways?

➢ Now choose your favourite two versions and write each into a single-page outline, complete with beginning, middle and end. Feel free to change the characters and plot events so the world naturally shapes the story. What happens? What do you like, and why? How are the worlds different, and how are they the same? Do they bring commercial or artistic appeal?

Beyond the sea

Exploring worlds isn't only about exploring the familiar or places you're already aware of. In drama there are a multitude of alternative realities waiting to be discovered. Choosing which might best fit your story means that you can go beyond your usual frame of reference. Setting a script in a new location will alter its events, atmosphere and energy, and it's always worth investigating not only the different worlds but also the possible realities it can inhabit.

Some scripts need more than one world, where conflict and thematic territory grow out of the way they combine and collide. It's therefore important not only to explore one world, but to investigate the relationship, conflicts and connections between the different worlds within a story. Working in this way can make a script dramatically potent and commercially appealing.

> *Grace and Stella are sisters but grew up without knowing each other. One day their paths cross and slowly they realise they're related. How will this affect them and what will they find in themselves upon meeting the other?*

➤ Think of five *naturalistic* worlds this story could be set in: specific locations, not general ones. Consider where they live or where they work, where they spend most of their everyday lives. How are the worlds of the sisters different, and how would the two worlds relate?

➤ Then think of five *imaginary* worlds for the story – not from real life as we know it, but unusual settings beyond the ordinary. Stretch the boundaries of your imagination and find new places they could inhabit. Again consider how each of them lives their daily life and what happens when their worlds collide.

➤ If Grace and Stella weren't humans, where could the story be set then?

➤ Choose your favourite worlds from the naturalistic and imaginary lists and write a short synopsis for the story set first in one, then the other. What dramatic possibilities are created by each of the locations? What ways could they combine?

➤ Now choose one of the naturalistic worlds for Grace and one of the imaginary worlds for Stella to see how further combinations of worlds might work.

Television set

Worlds are particularly significant in long-running TV series. Perhaps more than any form, the TV series hinges on a strong familiarity with and appeal of the setting. This is because the audience, watching on a regular basis, should want to spend time there; they should feel part of the world and have an affinity with its people. Stories and characters are still important, of course, but it's often the sense of place that prompts these into being.

➢ Choose a TV series and watch as many episodes as possible. If you can, watch different seasons so you see how the world remains constant, even if the characters don't. Then ask yourself the following:

- ○ What is the world of this series? What kind of place is it?
- ○ How big or small is the world? Is this significant to the series?
- ○ Does anyone own or control the world? If so, who and how?
- ○ How is the world divided up or segmented?
- ○ Which characters inhabit the world? Do they share it equally, or do they belong to different parts?
- ○ How do the characters feel about living in this world?
- ○ What types of story does the world allow? What types of story are denied?
- ○ If the world were a person, what kind of person would it be? Sketch out a brief biography.
- ○ Would you like to be part of the world? Why, or why not? Where in it would you belong?
- ○ If you took the world away, would the characters survive? How might they change?
- ○ If you took the world away, could the stories be told?
- ○ Overall, what is it about this world that symbolises the series theme? Why has it been chosen?

➢ If you're creating a TV series, use these questions as a basis for developing a world, one that audiences would want to be part of for many years to come.

Outside the comfort zone

Specific settings are often related to characters in different ways. One character may feel at home in a world, while another feels lost, angry or bored. By considering how main characters feel in different locations, a writer invites dramatic possibilities into the story in a natural, compelling way. This is the foundation of 'fish out of water' stories where the premise is centred on a protagonist placed in a world with which they're at odds. This technique can also be used in more subtle ways, both in plotlines or individual scene writing. By placing characters in a certain world, the writer also places them in certain emotional or physical situations that they have to face and interact with.

➤ Consider the worlds of this story:

> *Ulla's a mechanic working in her father's motorcycle business. She meets Chuck, who's looking for daredevil stunt-riders for his new TV show.*

➤ What happens if the new world Chuck invites Ulla into is:

   ○ A modern, fast-moving media circus full of suave superficial parties?

   ○ A demanding live show touring the world, pulling Ulla away from home?

   ○ A secret society of thrill-seekers who dare each other to take dangerous risks?

➤ Write a list of five worlds where Ulla could feel at home, and five that would make her feel uncomfortable, and why. Do the same for Chuck. Invent more information about the characters if you need to.

➤ Choose the world that most interests you for each of them, then put them together. What happens? What do you learn about how worlds affect characters, and how they force them to act and react? How do different worlds naturally create different kinds of character journeys through a story?

A whole new world

The same world can house a number of different angles or perspectives. Getting to know its many nuances can give the screenwriter ideas for turning the world on its head or repositioning it so that what is presented feels fresh, original and appealing. This is where small detail comes into play, finding the nook or cranny in the world to extract specifics from. Perspective is crucial here – finding the right part of the world to tell the story you want to tell. Finding a new angle to a well-worn world can intrigue an audience and open them to its possibilities.

➢ Take the following world:

> Material World *is a clothing manufacturer based in Birmingham, England. It's a medium-sized company, run by brothers Sam and Jonathan, who inherited the business from their father. They mainly manufacture clothes for UK-based high street retailers. It's a fairly friendly business, with about thirty employees whom Sam and Jonathan take pride in treating well. The premises are old but in good working order, apart from the occasional leak.*

➢ Using each of the following changes to the world, create five ideas for how the stories, feel and tone might take on a new perspective. Think carefully about how a minor change, set in the otherwise unchanged world, can have a dramatic impact on both the audience and the writer's imagination. Change only one element at a time; keep the rest of the world as it is.

1 Material World is an *alcoholic drinks* manufacturer . . .

2 . . . based in *Greenwich, New York.*

3 It's a *tiny company*, with about five employees.

4 It's run by *single-woman Tanya, who bought the business when it was on its knees.*

5 They mainly manufacture clothes for *international boutiques.*

6 It's a *fast-paced, competitive* business, and Sam and Jonathan like to *keep the employees on their toes.*

7 The premises are *recently purchased, with ultra-modern facilities for work and time out.*

➢ Taking these ideas as a basis, develop an idea for a one-off TV drama and write an outline in no more than 500 words.

➢ When you've done this, go back to the original world and think about how much it's moved on. Are your ideas more appealing? Have you found a fresh type of world? Test your ideas on a friend or colleague.

Playing by the rules

Every world works by its own set of innate rules and internal logic. By knowing the rules of a world, the writer can more easily create events that feel believable and make sense. For the audience to see what's at stake and what's possible in a world, they need to understand how it works. This is particularly the case if it's a non-naturalistic setting, but is important even with familiar, ordinary reality. For instance, what's the implicit agreement between a gang of friends? How does a workplace function? What are the laws governing rented accommodation? How do you survive in prison?

Understanding the basic rules of the world means the audience will know what to expect, which helps the writer orchestrate hopes, fears and other emotional reactions. Without knowing the rules, it's difficult to create either comedy or suspense, for example, as both need to function within a specific frame of reference.

➢ Consider what rules this story may need:

> *Twelve-year-old Camilla finds a girl ghost living in a ruined old play house in her garden. The ghost is scared and lonely and wants to find its way home. Unless Camilla helps it leave, the ghost will destroy Camilla's house and family.*

➢ Write a list of rules for both worlds, Camilla's home and the ghost's world. Think about what makes them similar and different, how they can overlap, help each other or conflict. For instance, what time does Camilla have to be in at night? Is she allowed to stay over with friends or not? What's the old play house used for in her world and how does it work? In the ghost world, think about how and when the ghost appears. What makes it come into contact with Camilla? Is it something she does, or does it happen at a certain time? How far can the ghost move from the play house? Can others see it? How come it's lost and how can it get home? Can the ghost touch Camilla or affect aspects in the physical world?

➢ Write the five most important rules for each world, and how the internal logic of each functions and affects the other. A world doesn't have to follow the logic of our everyday reality, as long as it has its own clear and consistent internal logic.

Opening doors

If a writer doesn't know a world too well, but feels it's the right one for the story, then live research can help. When you inhabit a world, your eyes are opened to how it works, and things that you never even thought of become apparent. Dramatic potential presents itself in new and surprising ways, and suddenly falls into place.

➢ Choose a world you don't know well at all, but that you want to write about. It could be any type of world, from a workplace to a public place or private space.

➢ Write a list of the things you know, or think you know, about this world. Now write a list of things you'd like to know about this world. Try to think both broadly and in detail. Consider what would be useful to know as a screenwriter.

➢ Now make a plan to get to know that world. This could involve a simple visit or a longer, more embedded stay. Obviously, some worlds are easier to access than others, but do all you can to get a real insight, preferably by visiting it but at the very least by getting to know people who inhabit it. It's important to experience the world first hand as much as possible, and not through films or books. If it's difficult to get access, think about a part of the world you could enter, or a place with similar situations or values.

➢ When you've done this – which may take some time – go back to your earlier lists and transfer things you didn't know but do now on to the 'things you know' list. Note down the ideas you've developed since inhabiting the world. Think about what you've seen, heard and felt, and how this can be applied to the following:

  o Stories

  o Characters

  o Themes

  o Settings

  o Dialogue

  o Objects

belongs together and in what world, who is an outsider and threatened or threatening, and how to express this through dialogue. By ensuring that there's some kind of cohesive voice to the world, the story will also feel more unique, believable and engaging.

Location, location, location

Working with worlds is a helpful storytelling tool not only in the macro perspective. Writers should constantly consider which location might be best for particular scenes. At this micro level, specific settings help to shape dramatic opportunities that clarify, energise and polish a script. Here it's not so much about changing the plot, as making sure that each building block is as good as it can be. Whatever world the larger story takes place in, individual scenes can be set in a wide variety of locations, turning a rather ordinary event into a memorable engaging moment.

➢ Consider this scene:

> *Siba and Disda are in the kitchen, arguing about their relationship. Siba feels that Disda's always on the telephone and more interested in talking to other people than she is in talking to him. Disda feels that Siba is too laid back – he takes their love for granted and doesn't appreciate her enough.*

➢ Rewrite the scene, setting it in the following locations. Keep the focus on arguing about the relationship.

   o At a deserted windswept beach.

   o In the queue to the cinema.

   o While on a rollercoaster at a funfair.

   o Driving to a funeral of a distant family relative.

➢ What happens to the scene? What natural elements does each location offer that help the storytelling? What other possible characters can be part of this location and affect the main characters? How does a location support or restrict a character, emotionally or physically? What tone or atmosphere is created?

➢ Now think of five other locations in which this scene could be set. Allow yourself to think beyond the obvious. Find settings that are imaginative but still fit with the purpose of the scene, creating your desired atmosphere and thematic subtext. Find one location that'll make it into a comedy, one that would work well as drama, and one for a thriller or mystery.

10 Exploring genre and form

Writing genre is about expectations, knowing what the audience wants or needs – or at least what they think they want or need. However, if we always get exactly what we want, it can be boring. In this way, genre is also about managing a balance between giving the audience satisfaction and surprise.

Why do genres exist? Cynics would argue that it's all about sales and audience figures, and optimists would say it's about creating satisfying audience experiences and achievable goals for the writer. Essentially, it's both. For the writer, genre requires careful consideration of story shape and type, character problem and journey, dramatic world and feel. Because there are so many genre elements to consider, right down to inciting incident, goal, type of conflict, and climax, it's essential to ensure you're using the right ingredients to bake the cake you want to serve.

There are also sub-genres and hybrid genres to consider, which can throw up all sorts of problems and opportunities. Putting two genres together can create an interesting and innovative script, but can also be risky, if the audience is uncomfortable with the combination.

Since genre is a huge arena, reference to it is made in many chapters of this book. In this chapter the focus is on understanding the nub of what genre is, and how as a writer you can work with and against it in your script projects.

Themes and dreams

Stories within a certain genre often deal with a similar kind of theme. The narrative landscape of a genre script isn't only to do with world and visual elements, but also with structure, story and character. What the protagonist dreams of (wants or wishes for) can be integral to the genre, and a particular kind of character fate is often explored: film noir is about betrayal and tragedy; westerns deal with heroism; and romances discuss ideas around relationships.

This isn't to say that a genre script has to conform fully to such expectations, but it's useful to be aware of them. Certain elements have to be included for a genre story to feel satisfying, otherwise the contract between audience and writer is stretched and can even be broken. Genre writing is about fulfilling, managing and subverting expectations, working with the themes of the genre and maybe even bringing a new perspective to it. Different forms hold different dramatic opportunities and demand different dramatic requirements. Therefore, if you choose to write a story in a particular genre, it'll often naturally shape the theme and character arc simply because those are the dramatic possibilities the genre offers.

➢ What happens to the theme *In every mistake lies the possibility of a new life* in the following genres? Invent a short storyline for each:

  o Road movie

  o Romantic comedy

  o Road movie romance

  o Action

  o Science fiction

➢ If the character's general dream is *I want to be free*, how could this be expressed in these genres? Write a short storyline for each:

  o Chick-flick

  o Crime mystery

  o Family film

  o Disaster movie

> In each instance, adjust both theme and dream so they suit the genre. What happens to them? How do they change? How do they stay the same? Compare how different genres take the theme and dream in different directions. Why do the genres affect the theme and dream in these ways?

Genre protagonists

Although most protagonists serve the same archetypal, psychological function, their actual execution will vary from genre to genre. Whether a renegade cop in a crime drama, a soul-searching musician in a road movie, or a bumbling bachelor in a romantic comedy, each genre sets its own expectations about what kind of character will lead the story and what their specific plot function will be. Archetypically, all protagonists share the same function of guiding the story and how it's experienced, but in terms of genre, they have specific plot drives: to save the world, to right a wrong, to grow and learn about adulthood, etc. Screenwriters may want to defy audience expectations and come up with a fresh alternative to their genre protagonist, but it's worth remembering that audiences have expectations that have to be met at some level.

> Take the following as the basis for a protagonist:

> *Sandie is thirty years old. She lives alone. She works for a local company and is in the process of buying her first property. She likes to spend weekends pursuing her hobby, and goes on holiday to the same place every year. Her brother's a famous film star.*

> Flesh out this protagonist in more detail for the following genres:

> o Thriller

> o Courtroom drama

> o Romantic comedy

> o Sports

> With each genre, think about what an audience might want out of Sandie as a protagonist, and what expectations she would have to fulfil. Questions to consider are:

- Why does she live alone?

- What kind of company does she work for?

- What role does she have in the company?

- What type of property is she buying?

- What's her hobby, and how did she get into it?

- Where's the holiday place, and why does she go there every year?

- How does she feel about her brother?

➢ Build the protagonist into a one-page character biography for each genre, giving the necessary details about Sandie and delving deeper into the hows and whys.

➢ Compare the different biographies to see how much variation there is between the genre-specific Sandies. Which character elements set up the basis for a thriller? How does the character description lend itself to a romantic comedy? In each genre, what's the direction of the character arc? How do the protagonist's details help to fulfil genre expectations, and in what ways could they go against the grain? What do you feel is the relationship between character and genre?

Home sweet home

Worlds are particularly important when writing genre scripts. Each milieu offers unique story possibilities, and the way they combine with genre and tone will determine the overall feel. Some locations are inherently funnier than others, some provide more opportunity for suspense and mystery. Colliding worlds can also be a great way to refresh genre – choosing a setting not normally associated with it but which nevertheless allows the story to work in an excitingly appropriate way. This exercise will help you to explore which worlds suit which genres, and what happens to an idea when you allow the world to help determine the genre.

➢ Consider the following premise of a long-running TV-series:

> *Sally Angel is detective to the stars. She's called in when bad things happen to celebrities. Sally can be trusted to keep secrets hush-hush and restore order while keeping the bloodhounds of the press at bay.*

> ➢ Which worlds could make this into a comedy series? Brainstorm five and choose the one that you think offers the best comedic possibilities and surprise.

> ➢ Which worlds would naturally fill the series with suspense? Brainstorm five and choose the one that offers the most thrills and dark mystery.

> ➢ Which worlds could make this feel like a drama? Brainstorm five and pick the one you feel offers the most relevant emotional depths and thematic landscapes.

> ➢ Finally, see if you can find a setting that allows both comedy and suspense. Is there a world that could combine different genres in an interesting way and make it feel fresh and surprising? Think about both Sally's own world and the worlds her cases take her into. What tone would it have and what would be distinctive about it? What specific stories could emerge for Sally to undertake?

Fitting the bill

Sometimes writers settle on a genre first, then try to find a story. But the story doesn't always fit. Not all ideas are suited to all genres, and this can be difficult if the writer is locked into a specific genre from the outset, unwilling to look at what's not working and adamantly squeeing a square peg into a round hole.

Some stories seem obvious. For a war movie, you need some kind of war. For a disaster movie, you need disaster. But it may be that the war movie is at its narrative heart really a romance, and the disaster movie a political satire. It can be very fruitful to apply the form of a genre on to a story to explore the best fit, in case it brings fresh ideas. Sometimes taking a drama and adding a genre dimension to it can give it a lift and make it unique.

But how do you tell if a script is in the most fitting genre? The most important thing is to work with the story itself and what it needs without being too preoccupied by genre requirements. Genre writing at its best inspires and supports – it should not hem the writing in. It's also crucial to learn as much as you can about the genre you think you're writing in, and examine the themes, character arcs, narrative structures and styles often found within it.

➢ Take your current script or story and isolate the following:

  ○ Character problem, want and need.

  ○ Character arc.

  ○ Narrative structure.

  ○ Theme.

➢ Write these elements only on a piece of paper and put the rest of the script away. Look at the essence of your story and try to forget everything else you know about it. What genre do you feel is suggested? What would fit with these building blocks? Write notes about ideas that come to you that you might want to try. Don't hold on too much to what you already have – be brave!

➢ Rewrite your story in a new or different genre. Do this at least three times, trying one genre at a time. Work only with the essential story-line, don't worry about details. Undress your theme, character arc and structure, then redress it to fit a different genre. It may be that you find a whole new wardrobe for your story that'll bring it to life. Or you may sense a shift in tone, or discover a subplot strand.

➢ Even if you feel uncomfortable writing genre films, it's good to try. Genre isn't about selling out, it's about making a script saleable and appealing in its form. Adding a genre element can bring renewed energy and excitement. Try these:

  ○ If you're writing a romance, try it as a buddy movie.

  ○ If you're writing a sci-fi, try it as a western.

  ○ If you're writing a ghost story, try it as an epic.

  ○ If you're writing a thriller, try it as horror.

  ○ If you're writing a comedy, try it as an action adventure.

Mix and match

If genre is approached as colour-by-numbers writing, where you simply fill in a template, it loses its shine. When the audience gets exactly what they've been waiting for, the tension between expectation and surprise is lost. The genre becomes stale and it inhibits rather than invigorates the story experience.

To avoid the danger of becoming too obvious, mixing genres can be a fruitful approach – not just rewriting one genre into another, but actively combining elements to bring the two together. Sometimes one may be the key narrative, the other genre adding flavour and sparkle. Sometimes they may be more evenly entwined, where they inform and motivate each other.

Mixing genres isn't without risk. Instead of appealing to twice as large an audience, you may appeal to none; the comedy takes away the suspense, the action flattens the romance. There has to be a purpose to the combination beyond mere sales figures. The genres have to fit with each other, and serve the essence of the idea. It's also important to keep some familiar elements and not make the film completely unrecognisable, since the frame of reference is then lost. Genre is always about the balance between surprise and expectation.

➤ Create three possible storylines for each of these combinations:

- ○ Romance and horror

- ○ Western and comedy

- ○ Children's and war

- ○ Chick-flick and action-adventure

➤ Which ideas flourished in the mix and which wilted? What's lost and gained with each combination? Where are the meeting points between the genres where they organically fertilise each other? What are the inherent risks of each pairing? How is the element of surprise balanced with expectations when the genres meet? Which other genre combinations would you like to try?

Setting the mood

Genre should be apparent on the page as well as on the screen. Reading a screenplay should evoke the same sense of tone and feel as watching the film. Apart from story shape and character, one good way of creating a sense of genre is through the language and rhythm of screen directions. This can showcase your skills in crafting screenplays that *feel* as well as read, where carefully-considered language makes the reader experience the screenplay as the audience would: scared, amused, cheated, etc.

➢ Rewrite the following bland screen direction to evoke a strong sense of the thriller:

> *Rebecca walks slowly through the park. She keeps to the path and doesn't look anywhere but in front of her.*
>
> *In the bushes, she hears a noise. She's scared but tries not to show it.*
>
> *She sees a lamp post ahead and really wants to get there as fast as she can. But she's worried that any sudden change in movement will lead to something bad.*
>
> *She searches in her coat pocket for her mobile phone and decides to call a friend. But as she dials the number, a cat runs out in front of her, causing her to drop the phone.*

Things you might want to consider when rewriting:

○ How might you break up the action into shorter or longer sentences and paragraphs?

○ Which verbs might you change?

○ How might the focus or point-of-view change from just Rebecca to her surroundings?

○ Might you make more reference to sound?

➢ Now have a go at rewriting it again, but this time in the style of a comedy thriller (parody, perhaps). Ask yourself the same questions, but this time try to make it funny rather than frightening. Feel free to add extra comedic elements if you wish.

➢ Finally, choose your own genre and write it again according to that genre's conventions.

It's no joke

Each genre has its own necessities and needs, its own risks and rewards. Some writers are inherently more skilled at particular genres. If you're going to write a comedy, you have to be funny. If you're writing a mystery, you have to create suspense. If you're writing drama or romance, you can't be afraid of emotion.

When writers embark on genre scripts, they need to take time to develop the skills needed for that particular genre. As well as a great story, it also has to deliver genre fundamentals: a comedy's only a comedy if it's funny; a thriller's only a thriller if it's frightening. This isn't only icing on the cake but part of the essential contract between writer and audience.

➤ Being funny is hard. Humour can be incredibly personal. What's hilarious to one can be distinctly dull to another. When writing comedy, commit to spending time honing the humour. Watch and analyse three films that make you laugh and feel similar to the kind of comedy you're writing. Watch each at least twice and ask the following questions:

- What's the problem in the story?
- What's the main character's situation?
- What world are they in?
- When do you laugh?
- Why do you laugh?
- When don't you laugh?
- Are there moments of pain? What are they? When do they come?

The idea here isn't to create a definitive list that will crack the secret of comedy for all time. Studying films is no sure-fire way to success, but it can help to focus and inspire the scripts you're working on.

➤ If writing a thriller or horror, watch and analyse three films that make you scared and feel similar in tone to what you're writing. Ask:

- What's the problem in the story?
- What's the main character's situation?
- What world are they in?
- When do you feel scared?
- Why do you feel scared?
- When don't you feel scared? When is there no tension?
- Are there light-hearted moments? What are they? When do they come?

➤ If you're writing in other genres, find your own set of questions for what feels important, then watch and analyse three films that feel similar to your script. This isn't about imitation, but making sure that the script will deliver on its genre promise.

Finding form

Just as genres have their own sets of expectations, so do forms. For example, a feature film has a clear expectation about the size and magnitude of the story told, which is very different to the scope of the story for a ten-minute short. Similarly, a one-off TV drama offers a different type of story than a six-part TV serial. When developing a project, it's crucial to consider the most appropriate form. You may have a burning ambition to write a feature, for example, but your story might better suit a TV series. You shouldn't take offence at this type of feedback; instead, work with it and reposition your expectations, or re-shape the story to make it fit your ambition.

This exercise is designed to test your story instincts in the context of form. It's not to say that some stories can't 'break the rules' in some way, but it helps to strengthen awareness of what form fits a story naturally.

➢ Look at the ideas below and for each decide if they would work best as a short film, feature, TV serial or TV series. If you feel the idea could fit more than one form, write a short outline or notes to explore the different shapes the idea would take in each. After the exercise, reflect on what it is that made you choose one form over another. How can you tell what fits?

○ *Following the lives of a group of medical professionals in a private hospital.*

○ *An ex-patient tries to sue a private hospital where she was (mis)treated, and uncovers some murky truths on her journey to doing so.*

○ *A street musician tries to raise £100 in a day so he can buy a new instrument.*

○ *A street musician dreams of a better life, so makes it his mission to get spotted and become a national star.*

○ *A struggling local netball team hatches a series of plans to avoid financial ruin and become respected in the community once more.*

○ *A struggling local netball team stuns the nation by landing a place in an international competition, yet must radically up their skills to stand any chance of winning.*

11 Enhancing scene writing

Having worked on the big building blocks of character, theme, structure and plot, writers sometimes plunge into the script and forget about improving their craft at a micro level. Good scene writing is something that can definitely be learned and improved, and can make the most ordinary story come alive. Bland, unexciting scene writing can make the best idea fall flat and languish by the wayside.

Understanding what makes a good scene and how to make it work for the script is a key aspect of improving the screenwriter's craft. It can be very rewarding work, since there are many simple techniques that provide powerful effects and quick results. Taking the time to examine the purpose of a scene and what it needs to achieve is an essential part of rewriting, helping you work through your script to see if it's really delivering what you hope for.

A scene can always be refined further, and this is often what'll make the difference in the end. Working at this micro level leaves the script specific rather than generic, and forces the writer to be true to their characters, world and plot.

Overall, scene writing isn't only about good dialogue or suitable visual storytelling. These two specific areas are treated in their respective chapters. In this chapter, the exercises go directly to the heart of scene writing, examining purpose, structure, rhythm, tempo and sound, to clarify how shaping and honing scenes is a major part of creating the overall narrative. Once you understand why a scene is in the story, you can look at how best to express it with dialogue and visuals. The following three chapters thus work together, and it's a good idea to mix exercises from them to develop an exceptional level of scene writing.

Fulfilling the function

'Scene purpose' is the reason a scene is in the screenplay. Every scene has to earn its keep, and knowing why it's there gives a clearer picture of the necessary story steps. Even if you like just to write and not to plan too much, this is essential work as it'll highlight both problems and causes. Clarifying scene purpose is the foundation of all script revision and it's difficult to do any other work without it.

A well-written scene often has more than one function. There's not a lot of room in a screenplay, and each moment has to be as resonant as possible. A single scene may give information, engage audience with character, create fear or hope, raise a question, and satisfy genre expectations. Not all scenes need the same ingredients, but what they have in common is that they must achieve multiple tasks.

➢ To practise finding scene purpose, watch a scene from a movie you know well and ask:

- o What's the main purpose of the scene?
- o What's the main external beat (physical plot)?
- o What's the main internal beat (emotional arc)?
- o Why's the scene needed in the story?
- o Why does it come at this point?
- o What other functions does it fulfil?
- o What information does it give?
- o How does it help or hinder the character?
- o How does it serve plot and theme?
- o How does it fit with genre or tone?

➢ Now ask the same questions of at least three of your own scenes. Also ask yourself if the scene is really needed. What would happen if you cut it? Try it and see! Is there another scene that could serve the purpose better? Can you combine two or more scenes into one so that they work harder and become more effective?

➢ The best way to achieve a defined sense of scene purpose is to write a step outline. This will help you look deeper into scenes and understand their functions. For more on this, see 'Step to the Beat' in Chapter 16.

The telling moment

Usually, scenes have a moment where something changes. It may be an action, reaction or decision. Maybe the character's faced with a truth; something is taken away or added; a relationship shifts; a character comes to an understanding, or makes a decision about what to do. The change can be little or large, obvious or subtle.

By embodying change, each scene allows the story to progress, rather than tread water. The changes function like miniature turning points, ensuring that fuel is added at each step, driving the journey on.

➢ Choose three scenes from a script you're working on, either a sequence or scenes from different parts of the screenplay. Look at where it starts and where it ends. What changes? How does the change affect plot, character and theme?

➢ If there's no discernible change, consider what could happen. What step does the character have to take or what insight do they have to reach? Brainstorm five possible changes and see which fits best. Experiment with changes provided by actions, reactions or decisions. Test different power-shifts between characters. Make the change happen to the character; then make the character cause the change.

➢ What's the pivotal point in each scene, and how does it fit into both the character's journey and the audience's journey through the story?

The deciding factor

Scenes gain momentum when the actions in them have been seeded well beforehand, and pushed so much that they become inevitable, possibly even a relief. In this way, single scenes often have the most power when they belong to a sequence – a chain reaction. To keep a scene strong, it's a good idea to go back to the decision that led to the action and make sure it's clear, well-defined and possesses enough magnitude to keep the audience in anticipation. Ultimately, if a character decides to do something that's beyond their normal behaviour, we need to believe in why they've done it – the pressure that's led to the action.

> This exercise is designed to make you think carefully about decision scenes and their pay-off action scene or scenes. Start with the following scenario:

> *Amanda rifles through her husband's coat pocket for his mobile phone, checking his calls list.*

> What might be her reason for this? What's happened earlier that's compelled her to do it?

> Create ten different reasons that Amanda might have for deciding to undertake this action. You may find it useful to think in terms of initial action (what happened to Amanda in the first place?), decision (why did Amanda decide to check the phone?) and pay-off action (Amanda checks the phone). Think of different story types and genres.

> From your list of ten, choose one and make another list, this time considering what another pay-off action might be. Other than checking her husband's phone, what else can Amanda decide to do? Again, think of different story types and genres.

> Finally, choose your favourite scenario and write a sequence of five to seven scenes that would tell the action, decision and pay-off scenes.

Scene structure

Screenwriters often jump straight into writing a scene without thinking about structure. In fact, scene structure is an essential tool; not only does it allow the beats of the story to be plotted effectively, it can make the reading of a screenplay much more fulfilling. Where and how the scene begins, develops, arcs and ends can affect the reader's sense of mood, rhythm and pace, allowing them to feel the scene as well as imagine it.

> Read the following possible scenes and consider how they might start, develop, arc (climax) and end. Map the structure in five story beats, shaping the journey of the scene through each beat. Think about what the theme or purpose of each scene is, and how the structure can best serve this.

James has chased Vince to the edge of a cliff. He wants to kill Vince, but knows deep down that it would be much more fulfilling if Vince killed himself. As he tries to goad him into suicide, Vince confesses that he did indeed kill James' wife Charlotte, but reveals that it was because she was pregnant and not willing to leave James. This is devastating news for James – totally unexpected. In the end, James decides that he's the one who must die.

Sophie and Emma attend a couples' counselling appointment. Neither wants to admit they're having doubts about their relationship. Instead, they try to put the blame on the other. The counsellor realises that they both love each other like mad, but because it's the first time each has been in a relationship with another woman, their fears of changing circumstances have overtaken their true feelings.

Leon, Nina and Harvey have all turned up at the wedding in fancy dress. They've got the wrong end of the stick completely. In front of the groom, best man, families and friends, they have to try and make an excuse about why they're wearing what they are. They really want to see the wedding and, with the bride only minutes away, have to convince her parents that they should be allowed into the church.

➢ When you've done this, go back to each scene and find two other ways of structuring it. How does the theme or purpose change?

Turn up the heat

The term *rising action* refers to situations which become more difficult or tense. It's useful both for forging plot and sculpting scenes. Creating interactive movement between problems and solutions within a scene dramatises what a character wants, what's at stake, or shifting power dynamics.

Rising action isn't simply turning up conflict for the sake of it. It also requires awareness of rhythm and emotional orchestration. Drama can be heightened by shifting tension, playing with the audience so they hold their breath or relax. In horror movies fear is intensified by inserting a seemingly safe moment, a 'lull before the storm', just before the moment of terror. Controlling temperature in this way is a useful technique for all genres as it creates conscious rhythm, and is a good skill to practise on a regular basis.

➢ Pick a scene from one of your scripts. Break it down into its separate beats and list each in a single sentence. Give every step a value between one and ten according to how dramatic it feels, one for the least tense, ten for the most.

➢ Look at the scene's rhythm and rising action and draw a curve to depict it. How does it look? Does it seem right? How can you bring more 'heat' into the scene? Can you turn the tension up or down to suit the purpose and tone of the scene? Where are the pauses and changes in tempo? Where do you hold your breath and where do you let it out?

This is good practice for both long and short scenes: sometimes there's a whole sequence of steps that build into rising action, sometimes in a short scene there may only be one or two moments. But if they fit the purpose, they can make a big difference. Remember that short scenes need improving too!

Complicating factors

Conflict is dramatic fuel. This is true both for overall plot and individual scenes. Screenwriting is a concentrated form of writing, where each scene must fulfil a number of functions and provide a lot of information in a short space of time. Rather than a character wanting something and easily receiving it, it's preferable to complicate a scene so it takes three or four steps for the character to get what they want.

Bringing more conflict into a scene in this way isn't about creating sensationalist drama. Each complicating factor allows the character to show what they want and need, how much they care about it, what they're able to do, what they've learned from previous steps, and how they're changing. Conflict within scenes is a vital dramatic element that provides opportunities to express plot, character arc and theme.

Increasing conflict in scenes is similar to the concept of rising action, but works more with content than form. Try combining this exercise with 'Turn Up the Heat' for a complete picture of working with conflict, rhythm and scene structure.

➢ Working with each of these scenarios in turn, devise five ways of complicating its action:

○ *Grizzwald needs to find the secret tunnel leading out of the prison.*

Scene purpose – be tense and fast; make the audience doubt he'll make it; show Grizzwald's skill and brains, but also his inability to trust.

○ *Carlos is finally ready to tell Romana he loves her, but she can't hear him.*

Scene purpose – create comedy; force shy Carlos to take action; show how crazy Carlos is about Romana; create doubt that Romana will believe him.

○ *Eight-year-old Rixy tries to get her diary back from the school bullies.*

Scene purpose – to push Rixy into starting to change her life; plant a seed of friendship between her and one of the bullies that will flourish by the end; make the reader wonder what Rixy's capable of.

➢ Look at each of your five ways complicating the scene, and test how they serve the scene purpose. Choose one you feel fits best, then consider how the character will react to this complication. What dramatic possibilities does it incite? Write five possible actions and reactions to it. How does each solution bring a new problem, and each problem a possible new solution? What does the complication offer to the character for their inner journey? What does it force them to face? Where does it take them? How does it create a chain reaction?

➢ Write each scene out in full using your chosen complications, actions and reactions. If it needs polishing, rewrite until you're happy. Reflect on what you've learned about conflict within scenes and how you want to work with this in your own scripts.

Topping and tailing

An essential part of rewriting is honing scenes down to make them as economical as possible, and frequently this requires trimming beginnings and endings. Not only does this reduce the amount of screen time needed to explore a scene, it intensifies the scene's power by hooking an audience in more quickly and leaving them on more of a dramatic pulse than if the scene went all the way to the full stop. It also helps to shape the rhythm and dramatic intrigue of a scene, where the choices serve the purpose of the scene and story. Commonly known as 'topping and tailing', this technique is one the screenwriter will do instinctively the more it's practised.

➢ Take a fairly lengthy scene from a screenplay you're writing and, in the middle of it, literally draw a horizontal line across the page.

➢ First of all, work above the line. Start where the line is and work upwards, reading each screen direction or line of dialogue in reverse order. Each time you move upwards, ask yourself, 'Is this needed for the scene to make sense? Could I start the scene here, or does it need more before this?' Keep working upwards until you reach a point where you feel the scene could start and still make sense. Score everything out above it.

➢ Do the same below the line, thinking about where you could end the scene yet still make sense. See how far down you have to go, and score everything out below it.

➢ Now look at the whole scene and see how much you've been able to cut out. You might need to make some tweaks to the directions or dialogue, but overall you'll have successfully tightened up your scene. Go through the whole script and do this with every scene as needed, using this powerful rewriting tool.

Crossing over

Scene transitions pull an audience in and out of a scene, and connect scenes together. Though transitions don't consist of the actual writing of words, they're a powerful screenwriting tool. This is structural fine-tuning – crafting items into the right order, creating hope, fear and expectation, and distilling rhythm and tempo.

It can be useful to think of scenes as sentences. Sometimes you may end a scene on a question, hooking the audience in to await the answer given in the following scene. Sometimes you end on a full stop, allowing the audience to breathe out and settle down. It all depends on the purpose of the scene (or sequence).

By working creatively with transitions, you generate drive and flow, making the story feel smooth rather than disjointed and separate. Good transitions can also clarify and deepen theme and subtext. It's a useful method for genre writing, as comparisons and contrasts between scenes can often heighten both comedy and suspense.

➢ Write these three scenes into a screenplay sequence of no more than two to three pages in total:

   ○ Fatima finds a letter left by missing boy August.

   ○ Fatima reads the letter.

   ○ Fatima decides to find August.

➢ Read the sequence and analyse how each of the scenes begins and ends. How is the audience invited into them and how are they pushed out? Look at the exact points of connection between the scenes. How does one ending bridge into another beginning? What information, feeling and tone do the transitions create?

➢ Now invent three other scene transitions for the same sequence. Think about alternative ways to begin and end the scenes; different moments at which they connect. Work in detail, considering images, dialogue, movement and sound. Test how transitions can create comedy, drama or suspense. Think about where the implied 'question marks' and 'full stops' come in the sequence, and what effect this has on meaning and rhythm.

Catching up

Entering scenes late – or, not at their natural beginning – is a good way of hooking the audience into the action. Instead of starting a scene where you'd imagine it would start – say a group of pupils entering a classroom – it's often more effective to start when things are already in motion – perhaps the pupils putting their hands up to answer a question. This invites the audience to play 'catch up' and engages them in the drama.

It can also be fun to play 'catch up' with a conversation, where the scene opens on a question or statement and the audience has to figure out what's already been said. The trick here is then to drip-feed the backstory into the conversation in natural and non-expository ways.

➢ Write a series of scenes with dialogue where you reveal the background to the conversation, yet keep the scene moving forward. The situation and start-line are provided below; your job is to reveal everything in no more than ten lines of dialogue. You're not allowed to say 'As I said . . . '

Premise: *Travis is telling Irena that his father has suffered a heart attack. He's just found out from his brother, whom he hasn't seen for three years. His brother's asked him to come home, but he's worried about the reception he'll get.*

Start line from Irena: '*I didn't know you had a brother.*'

Premise: *Suzie's telling her colleagues in the staff room that their nasty boss is a convicted criminal, who has spent two years inside for embezzlement at a former company. Suzie's deeply shocked, and has called everyone together to start a petition against him.*

Start line from Suzie: '*I, for one, refuse to work for someone like that.*'

Premise: *Zach's unsuccessfully trying to convince his two young children that Santa Claus does exist. They've caught him in a Santa outfit, stuffing presents under the tree. He's doing it because he feels guilty about drunkenly blurting out in the past that the Tooth Fairy's nothing but a scam devised by corporate giants.*

Start line from Zach's son: '*Then why the stupid suit that doesn't even fit?*'

12 Strengthening visual storytelling

Telling a story in images rather than words is one of the key principles that makes screenwriting different from other forms of creative writing. It may seem obvious, but can be difficult to achieve. This is because writing visually isn't just about placing a layer of imagery over the top of a ready-made scene; it's about going to the heart of the scene and building it visually through a set of actions and reactions.

Due to the nature of the film medium, scripts have to find ways of externally expressing what's going on internally in a character's thoughts or feelings. Working with external composition doesn't only suit the form, it has a much more powerful effect on the audience. Although it might seem clichéd, showing rather than telling encourages the audience to interact with the story and experience it for themselves rather than presenting them with a ready-made version of what they should feel and think.

Visual storytelling also ensures that a script is playable – that the meaning will be clear not only on the page, but on the screen. This isn't the task of the director, but the task of the writer. The director enhances what's on the page and manifests it in physical reality, but the writer has to ensure it's present in the first place.

Four essential tools help screenwriters to work visually in scenes, and these will be explored in various ways in the exercises to come: active verbs in scene description; working with environments to provide metaphorical backdrops and dramatic possibilities; body movement, physical reaction and relationship to the space; and employing objects to express power dynamics and inner motivation. It's highly recommended to do the following exercises not only in relation to a particular script, but as part of your regular writing practice.

Doing, not being

By using verbs rather than adjectives in scene description, the writer ensures that a situation can be expressed effectively on screen; it becomes 'playable'. Showing a character tearing up a photograph works on film, whereas a novel can use inner monologue about hating your appearance. The adjective in the description 'she's feeling rebellious' isn't straightforward to translate to screen, whereas a verb like 'she kicks over the chair' is active and inherently visual. By writing with verbs rather than adjectives scene description becomes more dynamic and dramatically direct.

Another reason for using verbs is that these often require fewer words, which is useful as screenwriting needs to be economical. Every word counts. Through a specific active verb, the description will immediately indicate a character's state of mind or motivation. One carefully chosen verb can express exactly what's going on – walking becomes much more evocative when such words as 'trot', 'drag your feet', 'skip', 'stalk', 'stroll', etc., are used to describe it, as each has its own precise emotional association.

➢ As an example, the descriptive non-playable sentence, *Lottie feels hesitant and shy about starting school*, is transformed with evocative action verbs: *Lottie hangs about the gates, watching other children sauntering in and chatting.*

➢ Repeat this with the following adjective-laden sentences. Write action-led scene directions to express the situation in a playable way. Don't rely on dialogue; use actions or reactions expressed through specific verbs.

  ○ *Kate feels annoyed with her aunt, who never listens to her. She wants her to know how hopelessly old-fashioned she is, and how superior Kate feels.*

  ○ *Conny's on his way to his leaving party at work. He has mixed feelings about it – the work is boring but he likes his colleagues. He's not sure if he's made the right decision.*

○ *Rinaldo's so tired of his children's bickering. He can't bear to be a single dad and is at the end of his tether. He feels guilty and angry with himself.*

➢ To finish, go over scenes in your own script and highlight any adjectives. Substitute specific verbs for them. Look out for sentences with 'feels' or 'is' in them. Express feelings through actions, reactions or movement. Writing with verbs does need practice, but is worth its weight in gold.

Walk the talk

To avoid wall-to-wall dialogue, give characters something to do in a scene. Whether small or significant, it can add both dramatic energy and deeper meaning. We rarely, in life, talk without doing something else, even if it's playing with a napkin or pacing about. It's the same for screenplay characters, though you can spend more time than in real life thinking about what they do as they speak, and what meaning it might bring to the scene. Giving characters something to do can actually make the dialogue stand out more, because the audience is visually engaged in the story. It also helps to create pace and rhythm, and means that subtext is easier to work with because there's a relationship between what characters say and do.

For example, if a couple washing dishes in the kitchen are having a row, you can underscore how they feel by giving them specific ways of washing the dishes. Scrubbing a plate until there's hardly a pattern left is very different from giving it a quick dip in the water, for example, and these actions tell us a lot about the characters and their situation.

➢ For each of the following, come up with five actions the characters might perform to enhance the dialogue. Think about the purpose of the scene: what's it trying to achieve? Think both credibly and symbolically, and see how far you can push the action without making it ridiculous or thematically clichéd.

○ *Polly and Arthur are in the garden. Polly's accusing Arthur of being naive and letting the financial advisor talk them into doing something they can't afford.*

○ *Harry and Graeme are on a date in a Mexican restaurant. They're both nervous but really like each other. They're both worried that things might turn sour, like they always seem to.*

○ *Yuko's in his apartment, on the phone to his mother. He doesn't know how to tell her that he's already spent all of his student loan.*

➢ Go back to your own screenplays and add a more dynamic visual landscape to scenes, deepening character, story and theme.

Swap shop

A very helpful method for telling stories visually is to introduce objects into a scene. Because they're concrete physical items, they can be handled and used, traded, given away, fought over or thrown aside. This helps to express power dynamics and status shifts within relationships. By interacting with an object, characters act, react and decide, and are given a physical means to convey what they feel inside. This also ensures that a scene becomes playable, and creates subtlety and subtext.

Objects can be special, valued items or general items found in the scene's location. They can possess symbolic value or be of momentary use. If a scene is dialogue-heavy, long, slow or over-obvious, giving characters objects to work with will often make the scene come alive.

➢ Consider this situation and how various objects could dramatise it:

Taigi and Benny work at the same bookstore. Taigi usually does the stocktaking and Benny talks to the customers. Taigi wonders how Benny really is; he doesn't talk much any more, and she's worried about him.

➢ Write four versions of a short scene where Taigi, Benny or both use one of the following objects to express their inner thoughts and feelings:

○ A dog.

○ A book Taigi borrowed from Benny last week.

○ The new carpet in the store.

○ Concert tickets that Benny tries to give to Taigi.

➢ Think about different ways the characters can use the items. What might it mean to them to have the object or not? Who does it most belong to? Which offers the most fitting dramatic opportunities through which the characters can express their inner and outer situation, while serving the purpose of the scene?

➢ Now invent three further objects that you'd like to use in the scene, and rewrite it with each. Try the same exercise with one of your own scenes. What makes an object usable in a screenplay? What moments or interaction does it articulate? What subtext does it imply?

Valued objects

Props aren't only useful as handy physical items to dramatise scenes. As well as giving an opportunity to externalise thoughts and emotions, a *valued object* can also demonstrate a character's inner motivations, what they care about and what they plan to do.

A valued object carries meaning throughout the story rather than simply appearing in a scene or two. It's often tied to plot, maybe even theme or inner journey, and can have symbolic value. Its main advantage is that it belongs to a character, either physically or emotionally. They want it, and will give a lot to have or keep it. Because it's treasured, other characters can use it to threaten, humiliate, tempt, bribe or enlighten that character. It becomes an external image of their inner values.

➢ Consider this character and valued object:

Ani has a special engraved knife in her bottom bureau drawer.

Ask yourself:

o What does it mean to her?

o Why is it valued? What's important about it?

o How does she use it? What other uses might it have?

o Where does it come from? How long has she had it?

o Who else could want it? Why?

o What might she trade it for, and under what circumstances?

o What other objects could be related to it?

➢ Write as much as you can, inventing whatever story you like. Then write a short scene, no more than half a page, showing in two or three actions an essential moment in Ani's relationship to the knife. You can add other characters if you wish.

> Finally, take a main character from one of your stories and brainstorm five major objects that could be of value to them, literally or thematically, and how they could be used to tell the story.

Say what you see

A useful exercise to sharpen your visual awareness is to create interesting ways of visually expressing character traits. Even if the results aren't used directly in your screenplay, the exercise will help to focus your mind on showing rather than telling.

> With each of the following character descriptions, think of a short purely visual sequence that depicts who the character is. Aim for five to seven scenes in each sequence, thinking in as much detail as you can and not using any dialogue.

> O *Tolu is creative, fun, liberal and very well-liked.*

> O *Scott is feeling very lost, dejected and confused at the moment.*

> O *Kylie's on top of the world since her boyfriend asked her to marry him.*

> O *Selina's lost everything that she's built up in her life, but still keeps thinking positively.*

> O *Max is generous and warm, but only because he likes to be the centre of attention.*

> Did you find this exercise easy or hard? Was there a difference in writing the characters with a 'but' in their character description? How did you manage to accommodate the 'but' element? Does it come across clearly in your sequence?

> Now turn the exercise around. This time, for each of the following scenarios, write three short possible character descriptions. In each create a description of the character as well as a reason why they might be like this. What do you learn from the images?

> O *Doug walks out of the newsagent's with today's local paper. He starts to look through the back pages, but suddenly screws it up and throws it in the bin.*

> O *Zadie runs on a treadmill in the gym. She's focused and determined. She ups the pace continually, not allowing the pain to show.*

o *Chad stands in the supermarket, facing a shelf full of tins. He looks slightly panicked. He picks a tomato soup, looks at it anxiously, then puts it back. He picks a tin of chicken soup and does the same. He repeats this with cream of mushroom and Scotch broth.*

Trading spaces

The space in which a scene is played out can have a huge effect not only on its look but on its dramatic potential: the events it can contain, the mood and atmosphere it creates, and whether it invites comedy, suspense or pathos. It's always worth exploring the best milieu for a scene, as it can make the difference between good and great. Setting events somewhere that is less obvious can also generate new valuable story moments.

➢ Using the locations of 1) a hospital waiting room, 2) a football pitch and 3) a shopping mall, write as much as you can about each, asking:

   o What kind of thing could happen here?

   o Who might be here?

   o Who doesn't belong here?

   o What private or public spheres does it offer?

   o What objects does it contain that could be used dramatically?

➢ Now take the following three situations and write a short scene for each in all the above locations. Keep the main point of the scene the same each time:

   o *A couple breaks up.*

   o *Gordon discovers that his best friend's betrayed him.*

   o *Joy, Hope and Faith compete to see who's the best pickpocket.*

➢ Look at what happens when the scene is set in different spaces. What differences and similarities are created? How does the situation change, in large or small ways? What becomes the most interesting or suitable location for the story as you see it?

Imprisoned

It can sometimes be productive to put characters in places where they don't feel comfortable or at home. The pressure and conflict between character and space can make things happen, as the character is forced to act or react. By placing them in such a space, the writer can also open up a character and find out more about them, allowing them to interact with a challenging, alien environment.

➢ Take a character you're currently working on. Brainstorm ten possible spaces they'd hate to be in. Pick the three most interesting, and place your character in each, one at a time.

➢ What do they do? Who do they meet? What makes them stay there? How can they leave? How can each space help the character to progress through their inner journey? How does it help or hinder them? What significance or symbolic value could this have for the story and its theme? Choose the location you like best and see how you can use it in your script.

I spy

Writing visually is about revealing and creating perspective. The screenwriter hones in on something that's part of a bigger visual possibility, and the choice of what's seen – what's being focused on – is driven by the screenwriter's perspective on the story and situation. In this way, it's about focusing on what feels right and relevant to a story – finding moments in a visual landscape that best capture the themes being explored. For example, if the intention is to depict that, despite all the communication available at our fingertips, there's still a lot of loneliness in the world, what's chosen to visualise this is the result of the screenwriter's perspective on a situation – a situation that might be seen and worked with very differently by another writer. In this example, a scene might be depicted as:

> A busy internet café, where people sit at their machines and chat through webcams and microphones, but don't speak to their real-life café neighbours. The café owner washes cups, alone, staring at the wall.

Or:

> Parents standing outside a creche, waiting for their children. The parents talk on their mobile phones or send emails through smart

technology. The children come out in pairs, holding hands and happily chatting away to each other.

➤ Each chosen image helps to create the meaning of the whole. Whatever the scenario, it's the job of the screenwriter to find some element in the visual landscape that will communicate their perspective.

➤ When you next go out, look around for a scenario that catches your eye. Whether it's something interesting that's happening or something you've not encountered before, take a look at what's going on. Choose three scenarios, ideally quite different ones.

➤ With each, keep the original situation but shift it around to generate three different perspectives on what's going on. Think about themes and emotions, allowing them to guide your perspective. You might need to add or remove characters, reposition objects and change some of the specific details of the scene.

➤ When you've done this, write a short statement for each about how the scene is supposed to depict the different perspectives. Defend to yourself how the elements of the scene you've focused on support the perspective taken; the more you force yourself to articulate your thoughts, the better your understanding of scene composition will be.

➤ Finally, test your ideas on a friend or colleague. It could be a fun follow-up exercise to give them the short statements and ask them to match them with the visual compositions you've created.

Compare and contrast

Mirroring scenes allow writers to show rather than tell; suggest rather than state. Comparing and contrasting similar spaces through the narrative creates meaning and depth. As these visual moments recur during the story, the audience sees what changes and what stays the same. This acts as visual subtext, providing information about how a character is developing, what state they're in, and what their hopes and fears are. It's a powerful technique that helps the writer say a lot without relying on dialogue.

➤ Invent a basic storyline based on this situation:

> *Dalilla often visits the nearby café, where she writes her diary, watches the world go by, and sizes up the local talent to see if there's anyone worth asking out on a date. She's on friendly terms with the owner, and sees the café as a home away from home.*

➤ Write three scenes showing Dalilla at different times in the café – one at the beginning, one at the end, one in between. Make sure there's a change in Dalilla in each scene, and express this through her relationship to the space. Consider how this articulates her situation and arc. Ask yourself:

○ How does Dalilla feel different in the space at different times?

○ How does she behave differently or use the space in a different way?

○ How does the space look or feel different? Does it have different objects or people in it?

➤ What information do the mirror scenes provide in relation to each other? Do they say what you intend? How could this be done better? How is meaning created through comparing and contrasting the scenes in ways that support the story and feel cinematic?

➤ Try the exercise again with a character from your own script, either using an existing location or brainstorming three new ones that could offer relevant dramatic opportunities.

Visual pleasure

Although visuals can be pleasing in and of themselves, their main purpose is to help tell the story in a way that feels satisfying and relevant. Here, the idea of visual pleasure comes from the audience being shown what they've been expecting, whether it's something general such as the visual components of a genre's narrative, or something specific like the obligatory scene: a moment, usually towards the end of the screenplay, that's been anticipated through careful planting throughout the story. Either way, it's common for the audience almost to crave seeing a specific action, object, setting or location, triggering visual pleasure.

➢ With each of the following scenarios, create five ways to give an audience visual pleasure through an obligatory scene or sequence. Describe the scene or sequence that you think the audience is waiting for, and consider actions, objects, settings or locations that could make it effective.

> *Charlotte has a fear of flying. She's been attending a special course to get over her fear. She doesn't want to be tied down any more; she wants to experience more in life.*
>
> *Becca's allowed herself to be ruled by her boyfriend. Her friends can't believe how much she's changed. She desperately wants the courage to be able to break free.*
>
> *William has been working hard for years to become a primary school teacher. He's had a lot of setbacks, each one pushing him further and further away from his dream.*
>
> *Kurt's been biding his time with the Sheriff, but knows that soon enough his dodgy deals need exposing. He wants to show the community how power can corrupt people.*
>
> *Lisa and Brad have had an awful time camping. The weather's been rubbish and the tension's been unbearable. Will they admit their feelings for each other, though? Or are they too tired and annoyed even to think about it properly?*

Sound and vision

Visual storytelling isn't only adding pictures to a scene. It's also thinking creatively around the interplay of images with dialogue. How spoken words relate to what is seen can create subtext, mystery, intrigue, comedy or empathy. Dialogue and visual storytelling shouldn't simply echo or replay each other, but combine as a dramatic exchange and through this create information neither could give on their own.

One way to work with the interrelationship of images and words is by characters saying one thing but doing another. There can be many reasons for this: characters can be confused, lying, shy, scared, unaware or trying to impress. On screen, actions often have more impact than dialogue, which affects how an audience will read the situation. A good writer can play with such assumptions and create layered, subtle drama through various kinds of dialogue–image juxtapositions.

➤ Write a scene from the following situation and think about different ways that words and pictures can combine:

> *Felix, Robert and Ashia are in a nightclub. They all know each other. Robert really likes Ashia and is hoping tonight's the night he'll finally ask her out. He doesn't know she recently had a short affair with Felix, which ended abruptly after Ashia caught him mocking her.*

➤ Write three different versions in which Robert asks Ashia out and Felix listens:

- ○ They both mean what they say.
- ○ One of them is lying.
- ○ Both are lying.

➤ Think about what you can show through the way the characters move and use physical space, how they behave with each other and use body language, and how this relates to their verbal exchanges.

➤ How do dialogue and visual action combine in the different scenes? How do characters reveal their inner motivations or ambivalences? How do they get others to believe them? What effect does Felix, or other people nearby, have on the scene in each version? Is subtext created through the combination of pictures and words? If so, what is it saying and how does it work?

Seen and not heard

Screenplays can become cluttered with redundant words and speeches. Writers need to remember they're writing for a visual medium, where the currency is about expressing internal emotion through external means. For example, action, movement, gesture and intonation can convincingly express dialogue such as 'Oh well,' 'Really?' and 'You're kidding!' In fact, in screenwriting it's more satisfying to see people's reactions than hear them, the writing creating audience engagement through strong visual plotting – the pain in someone's face; the joy in someone's eyes; the fear in someone's movement. Using active verbs (movement), objects (symbolism), blocking or body language (relationship) and environment (mood) can be good ways of externalising the internal.

➢ Come up with five ways for each of the following emotional reactions to be expressed visually. Think creatively as well as credibly, and feel free to add a specific world or setting that might enhance the storytelling:

○ *Svetlana's overjoyed to see her mother after two years.*

○ *Colin's just remembered that he's forgotten to pick up his child.*

○ *Resh doesn't believe what the boss is telling him.*

○ *Evan wants to go into the bar, but is nervous.*

○ *Elouise is feeling really hungover, but must carry on teaching her class.*

○ *Nicola's having sex with her husband, but feeling guilty about cheating on him.*

○ *Paraic chats to his friend in the street, but desperately needs to get home.*

○ *Liam eats breakfast but is worried about his driving test.*

○ *Aisling has just heard that her best friend has died.*

○ *Yana cleans the house, as instructed, but secretly wants to trash the place.*

➢ When you've found five reactions for each, see how many fall into the categories mentioned: active verbs, objects, blocking or body language, environment. If there's an imbalance, try to replace some so that you're using all the different visual tools.

➢ Finally, go back to one of your own scripts and see how many times you can replace dialogue with a visual depiction, enhancing the internal through focusing on the external.

Show, don't tell

Visual storytelling isn't always preferable to dialogue, but has a lot to offer. It's a skill that requires training, and the more you do it, the more natural a screenwriter you become. By occasionally forcing yourself to tell a story only through images you break through boundaries and learn more about what's possible. When you later come to write actual script pages, this will feel logical and instinctive. The following can be a demanding exercise but is very useful to practise.

The creative screenwriter

➢ Take the situations below and, one at a time, write a sequence of three or four scenes. These should only use visual storytelling – no dialogue or voiceover. Think about which story beats to include, then find ways to express them with verbs, objects, locations, body language and movement (make sure it doesn't become mime!). You should be telling the story in a dramatic, believable and effective way. You may not be able to convey every detail, but the visuals should depict the situation and create the right mood.

○ *Robin tries to rescue his friend from a mountainside path.*

○ *Ruth wants to apologise for abandoning her child.*

○ *Akiko finds she's entered the men's changing room instead of the women's.*

➢ Read the scenes again and see whether you absolutely need to add lines of dialogue to make sense. What happens when you stop relying on verbal exchanges? What interesting visual moments are created?

➢ Go over scenes from your own screenplay to see if you can strip out unnecessary dialogue and replace it with more powerful visual storytelling.

13 Improving dialogue

Character speech can often make or break an otherwise good script. Novice writers sometimes write too much in their own voice instead of in their characters', or think that dialogue is about providing facts and information rather than expressing values and emotions. Good dialogue should suit the character, situation and overall story, bearing in mind genre, tone, world and purpose. Although some writers might have a natural ear for dialogue, as with everything else in screenwriting it's possible to train and improve this skill.

Essentially, dialogue is an exchange between characters. It's based on want and need, and increases understanding about the state of a relationship or inner feelings. The exercises in this chapter will help you move away from the idea of dialogue-as-content towards an understanding of dialogue-as-exchange, where what's important is both content and context. Good dialogue addresses not just what people say, but how they say it, to whom and why. Dialogue is thus about repression as well as expression.

Though important, dialogue is only a small part of writing a script, and is worked with mainly when polishing later drafts. An exception to this is when dialogue provides a way of deepening the writer's connection to their characters. Listening to their voices and hearing how they talk to others can be a doorway into the inner self, and a way for the writer to understand their characters better.

The exercises in this chapter will take you through key aspects of writing effective dialogue by looking at individual character voices, what happens to dialogue when characters meet, and how to work with exposition, subtext and key phrases. They'll also guide you in creating a productive partnership between picture and the spoken word.

Through their eyes

A key ingredient to creating good dialogue is finding a distinctive voice for each character. Sometimes characters end up sounding very similar, or as if they're all speaking in the writer's voice. Finding a distinctive voice isn't a matter of making up ways of speaking you think a character would use; it's something to grow from the inside out, and is ideally something you should discover, not create.

Writing monologues is an excellent way to begin to hear the voices of different characters. It by-passes too much thinking and creates an immediate connection between writer and character. Free-writing in the first person allows you to step into a character's shoes and hear them speak as themselves.

At the beginning it might sound like you writing, but if you do it for at least twenty minutes without stopping you should hear the character's voice coming through. It's crucial that you write the monologue in first person (as 'I', not 'he' or 'she'); don't worry about screen format, simply write in free prose.

➢ To warm up, write a first person monologue for each of these two characters: *May, twenty-one, a bus conductor, and Rohan, fifty-eight, a bus passenger.* Do two or three pages of free-writing for each, describing the same event from their differing perspectives:

- ○ Witnessing a traffic accident.

- ○ Having an argument over paying the ticket.

- ○ Waiting in a bus queue.

➢ How do the different accounts describe what they saw or experienced? What's similar or different about them? What's distinctive about their voices? Even though you didn't know these characters before this exercise, see what you learn about them and how they speak to you. What's revealed through their use of vocabulary, rhythm and attitude?

➢ Now choose at least two characters from one of your scripts. Pick an event in the story, a major event or one that feels important in some way, that you want to explore further. Write a first-person monologue in two or three pages of each character's view or experience of that event. Don't think too much, just let the words flow and allow the characters to speak. Don't put words into their mouths; just listen and write.

➢ Ask yourself how they experienced the event. Were they part of it or did they hear about it? What do they think of it, how do they react to it? How do they re-tell it, how does it seem in their eyes? What do you learn about them through the use of their voice? Do they have any particular words or ways of phrasing you can use in their dialogue in general?

➢ By writing about the same event from different perspectives you can compare and contrast their voices, attitudes and feelings. When you've finished writing all the monologues, read them aloud to yourself and ask:

o How are the voices different?

o How was their telling of the event different from each other?

o What was clear and specific about their voice? What surprised you about the way they spoke?

o What did you learn about your characters? Did you find out something new about their relationship or connection?

➢ How would you continue to develop their voice, through vocabulary, rhythm and attitude? Are there other key events or relationships in your story you'd like to write monologues about, to help you explore characters?

Guess who

Finding a character voice is exciting and inspiring, but sustaining it throughout a screenplay can be a challenge. This is because, unless you live with your characters for a substantial period of time, there's every chance you won't quite pick up on all their quirks. In real life, however, if we see people regularly, it's easier to get to know their voices.

This exercise probes the voices of people you know, so you can apply the principles to characters you're creating. It'll work better in a close-knit group, but can work in pairs.

➤ Take it in turns to ask one another a question that will require a long answer. The task for the one answering (verbally) is that they must do so in the voice of someone that they all/both know. Voice here means a person's style, pace, vocabulary and perspective, not their literal voice (sound). It might seem odd at first, but once you start, it'll become easier and enjoyable. Questions that you could ask each other include:

  o What does love mean to you?

  o Do you believe in ghosts?

  o What's the most rewarding thing you've ever done?

  o How would you spend a million pounds?

  o Do you believe in truth?

  o Where would you like to live, and why?

➤ Afterwards, discuss what it was that you heard in the voice. What made it obvious it was that person? What wasn't obvious? What worked, and what didn't? How might the elements of that voice be worked with further? What have you learned that can be applied to writing characters?

Speaking relations

Creating voices isn't just about characters in isolation. Nine times out of ten when characters speak, they are speaking to or with someone else. Even though we all have an essential voice of our own, it can change depending on who we're talking (or listening) to.

In this way, good dialogue can give the audience information not only about what kind of person a character is, but also about their different relationships. What do they feel about the person they're talking to? Do they like or despise them? Are they afraid of them; involved in power play; trying to impress them?

If you see dialogue as a way of revealing the state of play in a relationship, the less on-the-nose it often gets. Information and subtext will be revealed through the way characters speak to each other rather than in saying exactly what they mean. It's fascinating and often useful to see how a voice can change depending on who it's for.

➢ Write a short dialogue scene where *Bob talks to Peter about how he wants to leave home but hasn't told his parents yet.*

➢ Now write a short dialogue scene where *Bob talks to his parents, trying to find a way to tell them he wants to leave home.*

➢ Read through the two scenes and examine Bob's voice. What changes? What stays the same? Do the words he uses change? Does the speech pattern or attitude change? What do you learn about Bob through the way he communicates in the different situations?

➢ Now choose three scenes from your own script, ones with dialogue between your protagonist and at least two other characters. Read the scenes and ask yourself:

  o What do you learn about the characters through the way they talk?

  o What do you learn about the relationships in the scene through the way the characters talk?

  o Who in the scene has low status? Who has high status? Who drives the scene?

  o Is everybody telling the truth? Is anybody lying? Is there any disruption or interruption to the flow of questions, answers or responses?

This exercise is particularly interesting to do with a partner's script when you know nothing about the story or characters. It's fascinating how much can be revealed through a few short scenes about a character and their relationships.

Silent talk

Silence is a powerful tool for improving dialogue, and one that's often forgotten. Just because one character speaks, it doesn't mean another has to respond. A character's silence is part of how they speak, whether it's in their general voice and the way they relate to people, or whether it's expressing something in a particular situation.

> ➢ Rewrite one of your own scenes and make the characters silent for part or all of it. First choose one character as silent for the whole time. What happens to the dynamic of the relationship and the flow of the scene? Do other characters have to change their behaviour and speak differently to compensate for this? How does it affect them?

> ➢ Now try it with another character as silent. How does the scene or its meaning change? What do you discover about the the emotional exchange between characters? Can you make the scene move in interesting ways that feel relevant to theme, tone and genre? Go back and rewrite the scene in the way you feel it would work best, making use of silence where necessary. Try it with other scenes too.

Lying and denying

Often writers forget that characters don't have to answer a question or respond to another character just because they engage in conversation. In fact, by disrupting and interrupting the flow of dialogue you often create more dramatic tension, and evoke a desire to know more. Try holding back instead of spilling the beans to see what new complications and conflicts arise.

> *Rachel tells her girlfriend Rebecca about a new friend, Ria. Rebecca wants to know what they were doing and where they met.*

> ➢ First write this scene with Rachel answering all Rebecca's questions and responding to her comments.

> ➢ Then write the scene with Rachel lying, denying, ignoring or diverting Rebecca. Don't forget to use silence.

> ➢ How are the two scenes different? What are the interesting moments, exchanges or expressions? What happens to your understanding of the characters and their voices? What happens to the rhythm of the scene and the emotional dynamic of the relationship?

> ➢ Try rewriting a scene from your own script and make the characters lie to each other instead of telling the truth. Do this either by making both of them lie, or by taking turns. They don't have to be big lies connected to the plot. The rewrite can simply be about making the direction of the dialogue less straightforward to see what happens when you interrupt and disrupt it.

Writing subtext

Being asked to write subtext into a scene isn't easy; subtext should feel natural and organic to the characters and story, not forced or contrived. Nevertheless, because subtext is so powerful, and often tells us things about the characters and story that aren't obvious, it's a good idea to practise writing subtext so you understand it better. Whether a character is frightened, ignorant, shy, lying, manipulative, or embarrassed, using subtext is a powerful tool to reveal the true purpose of a scene.

A good way to practise subtext is to impose an agenda on to a given scenario. This gives the screenwriter a clear hidden agenda to follow, and much to think about in terms of crafting dialogue to suit.

➢ Write a scene for each of the following, without allowing the characters to say outright what they mean:

Situation: *Andrew's in a café, ordering a drink from the waitress, Minny.*

Subtext: *Andrew really fancies Minny. In fact, the only reason he comes into the café is because he wants to ask her out on a date.*

Situation: *Dr Mecham is talking to his receptionist, Gail, about plans for the surgery's redecoration.*

Subtext: *Dr Mecham wants Gail to know that he knows she's been snooping through patients' files and spreading rumours.*

Situation: *Larry's having afternoon tea with his friends Gerard and Olive, a married couple.*

Subtext: *Larry wants to find out if Gerard and Olive would be interested in having a threesome with him.*

➢ Choose a scene with at least two characters and plenty of dialogue from one of your screenplays. Keep the same basic setting and structure of the scene, but rewrite it with the following subtextual agendas. This will inevitably change the whole purpose of your scene, but it's more about trying to find ways of improving writing subtext than changing what your story's about.

○ Someone wants to make someone else feel very guilty.

○ Someone wants to assert their authority.

○ Someone wants to make it known that they've seen someone else being unfaithful.

Key phrase

A key phrase is a sentence or few words repeated throughout a story, often by the same person but sometimes by different characters. It can be a useful tool since each time it's spoken, it gathers impact and momentum, and the audience comes to have certain expectations of it. It can then be used as a shorthand way of creating dramatic tension, thematic meaning or emotion.

Key phrases are often connected to a story's deep theme and are an excellent way to express characters' essential problems or issues without stating them in an obvious way. It's interesting to track a key phrase through a script to see how it changes, how it's used, and what deeper meaning it brings to the character arc and theme.

➤ Choose a film you know well and watch it again to locate a key phrase. What is the phrase? How is it used, who is it spoken by and when? Does its meaning or use change during the story? What expectations does it create for the audience? How does the key phrase relate to the theme of the film and its central dramatic question?

➤ Look through one of your own scripts. Can you find a key phrase already being used by a character? If not, can you think of one? Consider your theme and what the emotional journey is. Which word, question or statement can sum this up in a way where it can also change and grow through the story? Create five different phrases and assess how they can be used by different characters at different times.

Exposition – creating a need to know

Exposition is information which the audience needs to know to make sense of the plot and relationships in a story. The problem is that the characters often already know this, so it's the audience that has to be told. However, scenes where characters impart information solely for the benefit of the audience can feel dry and unbelievable.

A certain amount of exposition is always necessary, but to make it dramatically valid it's good to place it somewhere in the story where there's a 'need to know' – a curiosity on the part of either character or audience so that they actively want to hear the information. It should also be placed where it has a dramatic impact and feels authentic. Questions are a good tool when writing exposition, especially if one character asks for information and another won't answer – then a natural 'need to know' is often created in the audience.

➤ Look at the following premise and consider its need for exposition:

> *Vera and her daughter Mary are going on a cruise holiday. While on the boat they meet Vera's ex and Mary's father, Clive.*

➤ The audience may need to know about Vera and Clive's former relationship: how long they were together, when they split up, why they split up. Obviously both Clive and Vera know the details already, so you'll need to find ways of imparting the information to the audience without sounding false or forced.

➤ Create a 'need to know' that makes either character or audience want to know what's happened in the past. For example:

○ *Mary's never been told the real reason why her father left, and now that she's seen him again she's trying to get the truth out of him.*

○ *Clive was never able to tell Mary why he left and now wants to, but Mary doesn't want to know.*

○ *Vera's made a new acquaintance on the cruise who's a real gossip and loves to sniff out juicy tidbits from other people's lives.*

○ *Clive and Vera pretend not to know each other, but when Mary has an accident Vera is forced to inform about the next of kin and that he's here.*

➤ Think of five more ways to create a 'need to know' for either the audience or other characters in this situation. It could involve using other characters or a new event. Consider what dramatic possibilities they contain for relaying essential backstory information to the audience.

Exposition – breaking it up

Allowing characters to tell the audience what needs to be told while something else is going on can inject more dramatic drive into a scene. It can mean giving characters something to do while talking, or that something happens to interrupt the talk, or that a situation allows the talk to be punctuated with comedy, tension or drama.

➤ Taking the situation from the previous exercise, with Mary, Vera and Clive on the cruise ship, think of ten ways to break up a rather long and boring conversation discussing the terms of custody for Mary. For instance, they could have the conversation while:

○ *Going bowling on the lower decks of the ferry.*

○ *Vera relaxes in the spa and Clive gatecrashes it fully clothed.*

○ *Mary plays the one-arm bandits and wins an avalanche of coins.*

○ *The emergency siren sounds and they're swept into a lifeboat drill.*

➢ Read through the possible versions and choose the three you like best. Write them as scenes to see how to make them work. Consider the most fitting dramatic possibilities for a genre, and what thematic resonance the background actions can give the conversation.

➢ Try this technique on scenes from your own scripts where there are long passages of dialogue.

Talking in tongues

Something that screenwriters often find challenging is how to write dialogue that doesn't sound formal and highly constructed. This is especially difficult for those also writing in other forms, such as journalism, public relations, business writing or student essays. What can happen is that what appears on the page is so well articulated it doesn't sound real – it sounds wooden and bland when it's not supposed to, devoid of rich character and voice.

When real people talk, they pause, backtrack, change tenses and repeat themselves. In scripts characters should also sound like real people talking, not delivering perfect speeches. It makes the scene sound more authentic as well as emphasising the moment and the emotion.

➢ Rewrite each of the following speeches, using the tools of pause, backtrack, changing tense and repetition. Keep the same start and end points, and the general purpose of the speech, but play around with the pace and rhythm to make it come alive.

> *'I will not be spoken to like that by someone like you. How dare you! Who do you think you're talking to? Did your parents teach you no manners? When you're in my classroom, you do as I say. Do you hear me? It's people like you who bring the name of the school down. Go back to your seat and get on with your work!'*

'Darling, what I'm trying to say is that ever since you came into my life, I've become a different person. I wasn't unhappy with the old me, but I wasn't happy with the old me either. Now I'm with you, I can see that the old me was awful. And that's why I want to make it more official. I love you so much. Will you marry me?'

'She had it coming. Right from the start, I knew it had to be done. The way she teased me was cruel. How could she think I wouldn't be hurt? I tried to cover it up and give her a second chance, but it never changed. She pushed me too far. You can see it was her fault, right?'

➢ Look at your own screenplay and think about who's delivering the lines under what circumstances, and tailor the dialogue accordingly. It can be helpful to read scenes aloud to gain a better sense of the voices at work.

The voice of the world

One of the joys of writing dialogue is that you can make the world you're writing about sound and feel authentic. Too often writers write in their own voice, or from the perspective of a world they know. With a specific screenplay world that is perhaps less known, the result can be unconvincing, even confusing. Therefore it's important to have a good sense of the place you're writing about, and how people in it talk to each other.

➢ Spend some time in a world that you're unfamiliar with, and listen to how it works. Make notes about how people speak, and how their words characterise the world. What elements make it not just an individual voice, but part of that world's voice? Listen out for:

- ○ Tone
- ○ Pace
- ○ Vocabulary
- ○ Jargon
- ○ Agenda/subtext

➢ Now think about what you've heard and write a mini 'dialogue style book' about the voice of this world. You might want to use the headings above to structure your observations. Write it for yourself primarily, but in a way that could be used by someone else wanting to write about that world.

➢ To apply your observations, write a short scene set in your world with the following premise:

Characters A and B talk about yesterday's events. Character C arrives and offers a different perspective of the events. Characters A and B try to change character C's mind so that they all agree.

14 Managing rewrites

Part of being a good creative screenwriter is managing the creative process. This is important not only at the beginning of a project, when generating ideas and creating characters, but also by understanding the whole arc and rhythm of writing scripts, and what's needed at each distinct stage of development.

In screenplays, the rewrite is openly acknowledged as an integral and unavoidable part of the process. Unlike prose fiction or playwriting, where writers are given greater free reign, a script usually necessitates a large number of drafts before it's even ready to be considered for production. This means that the screenwriter, more than any other writer, must know how to work effectively through each phase of the redrafting process, and understand the different opportunities and threats that present themselves through the many months, or years, of work.

Although all writers are different, there are some common challenges and problems that often emerge during rewriting. By being aware of what can happen, you'll be able to deal with it effectively and creatively, knowing that it's a natural part of the development process rather than panicking and assuming that something's drastically wrong.

Some of the exercises in this chapter refer to the rewriting process itself while others suggest specific writing techniques relevant to developing further drafts of a screenplay. Overall, the exercises will give you confidence to deal with feedback effectively so that what you're given can be reinvested productively into your project.

Reigniting the spark

Losing confidence and interest is one of the greatest and most common problems during the script development process. Writers need to keep trust and faith in their story, and not get disheartened by the time it's taking, by less-than-favourable feedback, or by seemingly insoluble plot problems. Another danger can be the sheer boredom of having to once again rework a story you've been writing for years. Wanting to get it over and done with isn't a good motivation while finishing a script.

It's not a passionate love affair: it's a long-term marriage where you make a commitment, for better or for worse. Late stages of development are a crucial time in a script's life, where you must remember why you want to tell the story and put everything into it, even if you're sick and tired of it. The more energy and heart a writer puts into their story, the more it will touch the audience.

➤ To reignite passion for a story, pick a project you're working on and answer the following questions honestly. Take the time you need, don't rush. You may need a few days to ponder:

○ What made you want to tell this story in the first place?

○ What's the most important thing in the story for you?

○ What do you really love about the characters?

○ What would happen if you never shared this story with the world?

○ How would you like the audience to feel when they watch it? What do you want to communicate, and why is this important?

➤ You may also like to try the exercise 'Falling in Love Again' in Chapter 15.

Give yourself a break

One of the most important things during rewriting is to create periods of time away from the script. Remember that breaks are a natural and essential part of writing. During breaks, the writing digests, is assimilated, and settles into new insights. Sometimes story problems are solved simply by giving yourself some time and space.

If you don't allow yourself breaks, your writing will eventually become ragged and wrung out. Breaks revitalise both story and writer, and should be respected as a vital aspect of all creative work. When planning your development schedule, be sure to factor in time for breaks.

o Keep a timetable of your writing pattern for a week. See if you build in breaks or not. How long do you work before you take a break? Try to find a rhythm between writing and relaxing that will sustain you.

o Allow yourself at least one or two days a week where you don't think about the story in any way. Every time your mind begins to work on it, stop yourself and put it away in a mental drawer, or make a note of the idea and then stop yourself thinking about it consciously.

o After finishing a draft, take proper time out. Put the script away and don't look at it for at least a week, preferably a month. Try to forget all about it. When you return for the next revision, you'll be fresher and more eager. Try to do this even, or especially, when under pressure of deadlines. This becomes even more important when you're working on specific scenes as you can easily become blind to their flaws and functions.

If you don't build breaks into your working day, your writing can actually become worse the more you work on it. It's quality, not quantity, that matters.

Filtering feedback

One of the problems with receiving feedback on your screenplay is that so much of it can be conflicting. One reader loves your protagonist, another may hate them; one reader loves your dialogue, another thinks it's bland. It can be very confusing, and rather than helping you to develop your work in an effective way, it can hinder progress and send you on a wild goose chase. There's also the danger that feedback can get personal – where comments have more to do with the writer than the project. In these cases, comments don't get to the root of the problem because readers are reacting to symptoms, not to the underlying cause.

Just as a script reader approaches screenplays objectively when writing a report, so should writers try to remain objective when reading and responding to feedback. Although it might be hard, because intrinsically the feedback can feel like a judgement on your abilities as a writer, try to distance yourself and think about it in a methodical and pragmatic way.

➢ Create a list of all the things you feel are most important when telling your story. This can be very personal, and from your point of view. Use broad headings, such as 'character', 'story/theme', 'narrative structure', 'dialogue' and 'visual grammar'. Write what feels important to you, and don't worry what might be right or wrong.

➢ Under each heading, write further notes about those things you think are important. They can be single words, statements, or even questions. For example, under the 'character' heading you might write:

○ They go through hell to get what they want.

○ At one point we should really doubt them.

○ Who's their one true friend, and what do they give to them?

○ Are they active enough in pursuing their goal, or are they carried along?

➢ Under the 'story/theme' heading, you might write:

○ There should always be hope.

○ Small invisible steps that suddenly lead to big change.

○ How's the emotion orchestrated through the plot structure?

○ Does the final sequence reinforce the central theme?

Breaking your story down in this way will help you filter the feedback you receive into areas you feel are relevant to the project. It also allows you to look at one aspect at a time with feedback drawn from a variety of readers, rather than dealing with a series of all-encompassing and potentially overwhelming reports.

Temptations

After working on a story for months, a new idea can feel like a godsend and the answer to all your prayers. The sheer newness of it spreads freshness and energy. It's like getting infatuated after years of everyday marriage and thinking that it's love. Of course new ideas found during rewriting can greatly improve a script, but beware of being seduced by a new idea simply because it's new, without exploring it more deeply to see if it really fits.

➢ If you're attracted to a big new idea or story strand in a project you're working on, test it against the following checklist to see if it's really the right path to follow:

○ How does the new idea fit with your central dramatic question?

○ Does the new idea resonate with the core theme of the story?

○ Does it take characters deeper into their journey and towards their need?

○ Does the new idea develop the plot with the right kind of obstacles?

○ How does it fit with the tone, style and genre of the projects?

➢ If you answer yes to all or most of the above, it's probably a suitable idea. If no, either drop it or think more about how to develop it so that it fits.

In certain cases, as a script progresses the central dramatic question and thematic core can change. This can be positive, taking the writer deeper into the reasons why they're writing the story. In such cases it's important to redefine the CDQ and CTQ so there's a clear, new compass to guide the rewrite, see 'Finding Your Compass' in Chapter 3.

Building blocks

A common mistake during rewriting is simply to trim and polish instead of really getting your hands dirty and doing major remodeling. Polishing is fine for later drafts, but in the early stages of development (maybe even up to drafts five to seven), it can be necessary to make big changes. Adding or removing characters, creating or losing plot points or changing structure can all make a huge difference and help solve thorny story issues.

It's very important that you dare to make big changes while rewriting, at least to test the story to see what happens. One of the biggest mistakes by new writers is to make hardly any revisions at all, and then call it a new draft.

To help you work with the potential of the rewriting process, try the following:

1 Find eight to ten key plot points of your script.

2 Write each plot point on an index card, describing it in one clear sentence: what happens, emotional reactions, what changes?

3 Lay out the cards and look at them.

4 Shift them around to create different narrative structures. Try this one at a time to see what happens to the story. Dare to do something radical and major: what happens if the last point comes first? Or swap two around? Or take some of them out?

➤ You may feel you know the order you want to tell the story in, but it's always worth testing other variations, if only to discover something you didn't know. You can also do this exercise with all the scenes in a sequence or act.

Working on cards in this way is invaluable during rewriting, where it's easy to get lost in a script and see only scene descriptions, dialogue and detail. Keeping the essence of the building blocks on cards and looking at how they relate to and affect each other gives an overview that allows the writer to focus on what's really going on.

Running out of fuel

A common problem in many scripts is that they run out of fuel half way through. By the time it gets to the midpoint, most of the plot is used up. It's also common that the story starts too early, so that the first half covers what's mainly backstory. This means that there's often not enough plot to sustain a whole feature (or TV series), and the story either runs out in the sand or begins to repeat itself.

To give a story enough fuel, make sure the character really wants what they're trying to achieve, then put increasingly difficult obstacles in their way. Something also needs to be at stake so that there's enough dramatic pressure and tension throughout. If you ensure that the midpoint affects the character in a powerful way that changes everything, a large enough problem is created to sustain the story through the remainder of the second act. Make sure it's also the right kind of problem in relation to both the CDQ and CTQ.

➤ Read the following first half of a story and brainstorm five possible midpoints that could propel the plot into a new direction that is potent enough to sustain the second half.

Cousins Elsa and Henry played together as kids but have not seen each other for over twenty years. When they meet at a family reunion, Elsa shares some terrible news. She's received an anonymous threatening letter. Henry pales. In a teenage game years ago, a friend was killed in what seemed like an accident but what was really Henry and Elsa's fault. No one knows but them – but now someone is after them. This could ruin their carefully built up lives and bring up what they tried to bury in the past. Elsa needs Henry to help her, and so draws him into a web of blackmail and intrigue. As the past comes back to haunt them, Henry begins to realise that maybe he never knew the whole truth of that terrible event.

➢ Find as many different kinds of midpoint as possible. Look at each and work out what they offer. How much new story is sparked off by the event? How relevant is it to the theme? Will it lead the character journeys in the right direction? Does it fit the genre? Does it set up any twists or surprises for the end? Does it provide enough fuel for the rest of the screenplay?

What's really going on?

As your script develops through numerous drafts and copious notes from a variety of people you can start to lose sight of the initial idea and whether it's being achieved. This isn't necessarily a bad thing; as the screenplay develops, so do your ideas and your feelings towards the story or characters. However, it's important not to lose sight of the idea that was driving you to write the story in the first place, because it may be that very idea that holds the real power. It's also important to remember that this is your screenplay, and by trying to please everyone who's given you development notes you might have changed the screenplay in ways that aren't really beneficial. At this point, it's a good idea to sit back and take stock of what you've got in the screenplay – or what you think you've got . . .

➢ Re-read your screenplay and ask yourself the questions below. When answering them, think about what you originally intended and if this is still clear in what you've written. If you feel you've deviated from your original intentions in the wrong way, make notes about what your intentions were and how you might reconnect to these. Be honest with yourself at all times, and don't be afraid to admit where you think you've taken a wrong turn.

- Who's the main character? What's their dramatic problem, and is there a clear emotional need that engages the audience in their journey?

- What themes come to mind as you read the screenplay? Are they the themes you had in mind when writing it?

- What was the strongest emotional reaction you felt when reading it again? Was this the one you expected? How did it feel?

- Was it easy or difficult to read the screenplay? What made it easy? What made it difficult?

- If you had to describe the screenplay in one sentence to a producer, what would it be?

- If you had to give a reason why a friend should read the screenplay, what would it be?

➢ Use this exercise for all your projects, to help you restore confidence and belief that you're achieving what you set out to achieve.

Rhythm and tempo

Narrative structure isn't only related to story content. Its form also has a major effect on the audience's emotions and helps to shape the cinematic experience. By paying attention to structure, a writer also pays attention to the rhythms the plot moves through. As in music, the tempo provides emotional cues and suggestions. A story doesn't only work as individual scenes, but has to make sense as a whole. At certain points it needs pace and intensity, then may need time to breathe and slow down.

Always consider action, reaction and decision scenes. A plot needs both action and time for that action to take effect. This is sometimes referred to as *aftermath scenes*. If a story follows the same tempo throughout even the most intense action-packed script becomes boring; it needs peaks and troughs so that dramatic contrast is created.

It's useful to think of scenes as sentences: is there a question, statement, answer, full stop, pause, new paragraph, exclamation mark? As you read your script, try to feel where it speeds up and where it slows down. What's the emotional impact of reading it?

> ➤ Read through your current draft. Use three differently coloured highlighter pens and make marks in the margin for each scene as you feel its tempo. Use one colour for fast, one for slow, and one for normal.

> ➤ Look at the colours. Is there a balance between them? Balance doesn't mean that all of them need to be in equal amounts, but rather that they're all present in some way.

> ➤ Now pick three major events in your story and write an aftermath scene for each, where the main character is alone, reflecting on or digesting what's happened, and in the process of deciding what to do next. Do you have enough aftermath scenes? Go through them and count them and find out where they're needed.

Collapsible cast

Early drafts of scripts sometimes have a huge cast of characters. During rewriting it's important to look at who you really need, and if there are better ways to use them. This will leave you with characters that make more of an impact, even if they're minor characters. It also helps to clarify the dramatic needs of scenes and relationships: who needs who?

> ➤ Choose two or three minor characters from your story and describe their key qualities and what they provide dramatically for the story. Think about what's essential and write this as a new list. Look at this list and create a single character that could encompass all of these qualities.

As an example, here is Vera with three possible minor characters for her story:

Vera, thirty-six, is a bored veterinarian. She longs for excitement, but is a shy, quiet person not used to welcoming adventure into her life.

- *Julie's a veterinary nurse who loves to gossip and asks Vera extremely personal questions in coffee breaks.*

- *Everett's the delivery driver who comes every week with medical supplies. On Mondays he always brags about his weekend exploits.*

- *Flo-Flo's a spoiled dachshund who creates mayhem for Vera as she refuses treatment.*

➤ It may be that all these minor characters can happily co-exist, but some of their dramatic functions overlap, since the main reason they're in the story is to create difficulty for Vera and open the door to adventure. To test if they're all needed, see what happens if they're collapsed into just one minor character:

> *Everett's the worried owner of Flo-Flo the spoiled dachshund, and regularly visits Vera. During treatments, he loves to gossip and find out about Vera's personal life. To get her to open up, he tells outrageous stories of his latest romantic entanglements.*

Although you keep both the dog and a human, they appear in scenes together and so count as one dramatic unit. Rather than having many characters all doing similar things, Everett is more fully developed and becomes memorable and more effective as a minor character.

It's not always possible or necessary to trim down the cast, but it can be a useful way of optimising what you have. It also has practical bonus implications, and is a good technique when producers ask writers for narrative ways to decrease the budget.

Stuck in the mud

'Story blindness' can be a common problem during rewriting. Something's not working in the script but your thinking around it has been worn into such a deep groove that you're totally stuck and can't find a way out. This can happen to even the best writers.

To get yourself unstuck, creative lists can be very effective. They're a great way to tackle thorny story problems, at whatever stage: idea forming, outlining, redrafting. The key is to identify what the core problem is that's not working, and what is the best question or issue to start a list about.

➤ Find an area of your script that isn't working – maybe a weak plot point, a character that doesn't feel authentic, or a fuzzy theme. Be clear about the specific problem you want to resolve.

➤ Now brainstorm a list of as many possible new solutions as you can think up and write them all down. Don't worry about whether they're good – just keep writing.

➤ In this example, *Eldina the paramedic is accused of reckless driving and endangering a patient's life.*

　○ Though this is the right plot point, the current way she's being reckless (driving) feels too obvious and needs to be more surprising. To find something better, brainstorm at least fifteen other ways that she could endanger a patient's life.

➤ Alternatively, the problem might be that Eldina gets out of her trouble too easily.

　○ So now brainstorm fifteen ways that the accusations could worsen and become more serious.

When working with lists, it's important to create as many possible variations as you can. Usually the first five to ten are obvious, then the quality deteriorates for a while but, as you continue, surprising and innovative ideas begin to emerge. This is a simple technique that's invaluable for creating high quality screenplays.

15 Perfecting the pitch

Pitching is about seeing the essence and heart of a story. Often pitching is dismissed as purely a selling tool that can cheapen a beautifully crafted script, but it shouldn't be viewed as a necessary evil. It does help when selling, but pitching isn't only about reducing a complex, rich tale into a pithy line or two. Rather, it's about identifying and retaining the essence of the story so it can be told and retold in a way that captures your intentions. If a producer buys your story, they have to pitch it to financiers, distributors and audiences. By developing a strong pitch, you're putting your story in their hands in a way that ensures it will remain true to itself, no matter who tells it.

Another reason why pitching is so valuable is that it reminds the writer of what they're trying to say. When you're in the midst of rewriting a 100-page screenplay for the eighth time, tinkering with dialogue detail and scene construction, it's easy to forget the bigger picture. By working on the pitch, you'll come back to the core engine that's driving everything in the story. The pitch will help to remind you why you're writing the script in the first place, and should keep you motivated through the toughest of times.

Being a highly concentrated form of the story, the pitch can sometimes make writers feel naked and vulnerable. There's nowhere to hide as you have to state clearly and openly what you're writing about, and it can feel like exposing your innermost secrets. This isn't an excuse to avoid it! Learning how to pitch can help you pin down your story and nail your colours to the mast. In the end, you can never hide what you want to say; writing is about expression and communication. Pitching will help you to stand by your story, loud and proud, articulating it confidently so others will hear what you have to say. It's nothing to be ashamed of.

Ideas can be pitched both verbally and in writing. There are good reasons for practising both: you need written outlines to send to producers, and prepared verbal pitches that you can draw on in the most unexpected of places. Either way, what makes the pitch good is the combination of tone and flavour used, and the content it draws from. Whether writing or speaking, strong, emotive language gives the reader or listener a solid sense of your idea in just a few words. This becomes more important in 'pitch-fest' events where dozens of writers might be vying for the attention of a single producer or financier.

Although you want a pitch to be memorable, it should never be about gimmicks and showing off. Pitching is always about going to the heart of the story and sharing it with enthusiasm, clarity and conviction. If you have a strong idea, a clear sense of what you want to say, and you've prepared your pitch using the exercises in this chapter, you might even begin to enjoy it! And although you may not get a sale or an option straight away, you're likely to get more out of meetings and build rewarding relationships that will eventually result in work.

Practice runs

It's an ironic fact of life that it's usually much easier to pitch other people's ideas than your own. It's easier to see them clearly, and not get caught up in detail. With our own stories there's a tendency to get lost and confused because it all feels so important; we're too close to it and too emotionally involved.

A good way to practise pitching is therefore to use existing films or other writers' stories. This helps you get a feel for what makes a good pitch, and how to express it in a clear, simple and powerful way.

➢ Choose a single protagonist feature film which you've seen and know. Watch it again if you can. Try to summarise the events in 50 to 100 words. Don't make it exciting, just relay the dry facts of the story.

➢ Look at the summary and see if you've left out anything important. A moment, question, theme or feeling? How can you add this in?

➢ Boil down the summary to fifty words which includes key aspects not only of plot but of the story as a whole. Try to capture the essence of the film in the very best way you can. Does the feeling of the pitch match the experience you had of watching the film? What's the difference between a summary of events and a pitch?

➢ Now choose a TV series or a less classically structured feature film. Make sure you've seen it and know it. Follow the steps above and first write a summary, then a pitch. If there's not a clear journey or obvious plot, what's the essence that unites the story? How can you pitch that?

➢ Compare the experience of pitching a single protagonist story with a more unconventional narrative or TV series. What are the differences? How can you apply what you've learned to pitching your own stories?

➢ Do this exercise as often as you can, to hone your skills and feel comfortable with pitching. You can also swap scripts or treatments with other writers, to pitch each other's stories. This isn't only good pitching practice, but also useful for hearing how another person perceives your story solely from the page, and if the screenplay is communicating what you intend.

The heart of the matter

One of the biggest dangers is when pitches, written or verbal, become too long and complicated. Too much detail is confusing and boring. Keeping the pitch simple makes it engaging and more memorable. This doesn't mean the story has to be simple – a script may be full of twists and turns, but the pitch isn't the time to go into these at length.

Pitching is about revealing the heart of the story, what it's really about. A good pitch will make someone want to know more. If the pitch achieves this, then it opens the door to getting a treatment or script read, and this is where the full story and the detail will be revealed.

➢ Locate the essential storytelling elements in your current script. Write down:

o Main characters: protagonist and antagonist, or three or four main characters.

o Main situation.

o Central dramatic issue or problem.

o What the main characters want or are trying to achieve.

o What's stopping them.

o What's at stake – what'll happen if they fail.

o Genre and world.

➢ Now form this information into the following basic narrative order:

> *A is trying to do B. If A doesn't succeed, C will happen. What does A have to do then?*

➢ Play around with the pieces until they fit and you feel it works. Sometimes this might seem a little dry and formulaic, but it's a place to start. Add in genre and world where it feels most appropriate; often a written pitch starts with stating the genre. Make sure you draw attention to the right aspects of the story. How does this formula help you reveal the heart of the story? What's still missing?

This exercise can be a way to find a powerful written logline (one-sentence story summary). It's also excellent preparation for a verbal pitch. Even if it ends up feeling simplistic, it helps to clarify major building blocks, which are useful when telling the story out loud. Don't be afraid of telling the story in its simplest, most essential form. This doesn't make it simplistic, it makes it clear – there's a big difference!

Even if the story doesn't follow a traditional three-act structure, this exercise works well. Think about what's important to the characters and what's at stake, if not dramatically then thematically. What will the question be for the audience as they embark on the story? What's the journey of the audience as they watch? Try to apply the pitching formula to your story even if you think it won't work. You may notice things you hadn't seen before that pull it all together.

Finding your focus

Pitching is all about focus – deciding which parts of a story will represent the whole. But it can sometimes be hard to know which are the right parts. If you've been working with your story for a long time, everything seems important and interrelated. So how can you tell what the key elements are?

If you've tried to create a pitch by using the previous exercise and it feels dry, lifeless or just a bit too neat and familiar, try this one to by-pass all the things a pitch 'should' be and find your own inner compass to what's truly important about your story. Here you gradually narrow down your focus in an intuitive, emotional way, not thinking about what's correct but what feels right. Do this exercise without thinking too much; simply discover what you feel is true. Do it one step at a time and don't think ahead.

1 Write your story as a single-page outline (see Chapter 16).

2 Read the outline. Use a highlighter pen to mark words and sentences that feel important or resonant – ones that jump out and catch your attention.

3 Using the highlighted sections as inspiration, write your story in ten sentences.

4 Now write your story in five sentences. This isn't writing a pitch, so don't worry about making it sound good; it's only to excavate its emotional focus.

5 Now write the story in three sentences. If you want, be aware of plot, theme and tone. Or if you prefer, just write what comes, even if it doesn't make sense.

6 Finally, write the story in one sentence. Don't think too much but flow through the process. This final sentence doesn't have to be one from the stages above, but can be a brand new one inspired by them. Try to find something that really sounds right for you, what you feel it's about rather than what you think it should be about.

➢ Read your final sentence and think about what it says. How does it relate to your story and theme? What do you like about it? How can you use this sentence?

An alternative approach is:

1 Write the beginning of your story in one sentence. What's the beginning essentially about? What happens? How does it feel?

2 Write the middle of your story in one sentence – the most important thing in it.

3 Write the end of your story as one sentence, summing up how it finishes.

4 Put these sentences together and see what this tells you about the journey of your story, and what's most important to you about each of the stages.

5 Write a pitch for your story based on what you find. Let it lie for a few days, then look at it again and see how you can tweak and improve it. Do this a few times until you feel happy with it.

Falling in love again

Agents, producers, directors, actors or whoever's listening to your pitch don't want to be spun a yarn. They don't want to think you want to tell this story; they want to *know* you want to tell this story. But how do you convince someone of this? Essentially, it's through a mixture of true passion and sincerity. Pitching is about creating a relationship with the person listening, so the last thing you want to do is turn them off with fakery and a lack of knowledge about your subject. After all, if you don't really believe in the project, who will?

This exercise will help you rediscover that feeling of passion you had about your story when you first embarked on writing it, and remind you why you really believe in it, why you want to tell it, and ultimately, why others should listen to it.

➢ Think back to when you first had the idea for the script you're currently writing. Step back from the actual story and think about where it came from. What inspired it? Where were you? How did you put the inspiration into action? Who encouraged you to write it? How did you feel? How would you feel if you never got to tell it?

➢ Write a love letter from the perspective of you having just 'met' your story idea. Be as gushing and over-the-top as you like; just make sure that it's clear where the idea came from (how you met), how you're feeling about it now you've met, and what you hope to get out of it in the future.

➢ Go through the letter and highlight any key points that stand out as being at the heart of your project. They might be emotional, experiential or situational. When you've done this, pull all the key points together into a summary.

➤ How can remembering why you want to tell this story help you to pitch it? What ideas do you get about how to pitch it? What's important for you to remember when you do pitch it? What's the fuel that this love letter provides?

➤ You might not use exact words or phrases from the letter, but you should at least be inspired by them and keep them as the core driving force of your project. You might like to refer back to the summary every time you start to doubt your project or lose confidence in your ability to write it. This will act as a great reminder of why you fell in love with the idea in the first place, and why it should be pursued.

Pitching the right note

Pitching isn't only telling someone what happens – it's also speaking to them on a subconscious level, about what to expect when they enter the world of the story. By using the right combination of words and tone, you create a reaction in the listener or reader. This is particularly important with genre scripts. It's not enough to describe something as funny or scary, you have to make people feel it. Therefore the same story can be pitched in different 'notes' depending on its presumed genre.

➤ Consider what 'notes' are important when pitching the following story:

> *Diego works in a bar. At night he often sees shady dealings but usually pretty small-time stuff. One night after closing he stumbles on a drug mafia meeting. They discover and threaten him. Realising he's in danger, he grabs his bag and runs. He flees across the country, but the mafia are on his trail. Not only is he a witness, he has also by accident picked up their drug stash. They pursue him and he has to run and hide. He contacts the police but none of them believe him – apart from FBI agent Angela. Diego has to use all his wiley means to stay alive. His pursuers are not going to give up, so he has to put a stop to it. He creates a dangerous trap with himself as bait. The gangsters are about to kill him when they realise they've been set up. Angela rescues Diego and puts the villains behind bars. Diego finds himself with a new identity as well as a new life together with Angela.*

➤ Write a pitch of seventy words or less for this story. Use the given plot as well as your own ideas. Don't change the story, but use the pitch to emphasise how you want to tell it.

> ➤ Now pitch three further versions of the idea, using the genres of comedy, drama, and thriller. Use the same essential plot and premise but create different notes in each, working with tone, feeling, rhythm, vocabulary and key plot selling points.

> ➤ Compare the four pitches. How are they different? What expectations do they create? What makes something funny, thrilling or moving? How did you *evoke* that feeling rather than tell it? What makes it real and what makes it fake?

The spoken word

It's important to practise pitching both on the page and face to face. Written pitches need to be honed and polished, every word chosen with care. In the verbal pitch, clarity and attitude are more important than perfect prose – how you present the story with voice, presence and body language. It can be nerve-wracking pitching to a producer, especially when there's a lot at stake, so it's necessary to first practise telling the story out loud. You may think you know it inside out, but when you open your mouth even the best can get tongue-tied.

Verbal pitching isn't the same as reading from a piece of paper. It's about telling a story to a listener. The worst verbal pitch is stiff and rehearsed. The best is personal and in the moment, a real conversation with a specific listener, where the writer is clear, confident and passionate.

Every time a story is pitched verbally, it will change. Each situation is different, each listener is different. Allow the pitch to come alive: don't force it to be like it was last time, and don't expect similar reactions. Be present and allow the story to be told the way it is today. Be aware of the listener's reactions and how best to respond to them.

> ➤ This exercise will help you voice your story by speaking it out loud. Do the preparatory pitch exercises in this chapter before you begin, to establish a clear sense of what you want to say. You'll need the same essential information as you do for a written pitch, so make sure you know what your story's about.

> ➤ Over a week, pitch the story you're currently working on at least once a day, more if you can. Tell it to different kinds of people, in different situations – not just film people, but in ordinary everyday situations.

> ➤ During the week, keep a journal of thoughts and feelings recorded after each pitch. What was it like? How did you feel? What interested

the listener? Did you bore or confuse them at any point? What did you hear in the story that felt different? What did you learn?

➢ At the end of the week, read through the journal and summarise your main points. What have you most learned about pitching live? What areas are you strong in? What areas do you need more practice in? What's the next step to improving your pitching skills? What in this particular story needs always to be included when telling it?

➢ Repeat this exercise some months later with another story. Keep a journal again, and compare what you learn from pitching this story in relation to the first.

We constantly learn and improve, and pitching is about dedicated practice. Getting to the point where you're comfortable, clear and confident with a story is vital. It also helps to think of pitching as fun – not as selling or being under pressure, but simply as a chance to tell someone a story. What could be better than that?

The question is . . .

When pitching verbally, it's a good idea to start with a question. Questions are engaging, they arouse curiosity and involve the listener, hooking them in and inviting them to connect with the story. Like all aspects of verbal pitching, it needs to feel real, natural and authentic, not forced, fake or overdone.

A good starting point is to consider the central dramatic question that lies at the heart of the story. By allowing the CDQ to help direct the pitch, you make the listener want to know what happens. By using the central thematic question (CTQ) you show them why they should care. Starting with these questions puts the listener into the heart, both of the action and the protagonist's emotional journey, creating an affinity between the listener and your characters.

➢ Do the 'Finding your Compass' exercise in Chapter 3 to find the CDQ and CTQ of one of your stories. Then list ten questions that relate to the CDQ. Read through and pick three that resonate with you and feel most relevant for your story.

➢ For instance, if the CDQ is *Will Mabel find her real family?* good questions to begin a pitch conversation are:

- *How would you feel if you suddenly discovered you'd been adopted and no one in your family is who you thought they were?*

- *How far would you go to find your lost mother, even if it meant cutting off everyone you loved?*

➤ Now write down the CTQ and list ten questions relating to this. Read through and pick three that resonate with you and feel most relevant for the story.

➤ For instance, if the CTQ is *Will Mabel learn what a real family means?* good questions to begin a pitch conversation are:

- *Have you ever felt alone and disconnected from everyone, even your own family?*

- *Do you know anyone who has a totally happy relationship with their family?*

Using the CTQ as a starting point can be useful if you have a story without a single protagonist. Whatever the story structure, the CTQ is the unifying factor pulling all the threads together. Exploring pitching through these two questions will help you find a dynamic starting point for the conversation that ensures you'll have the attention of your listener.

16

Building outlines and treatments

During the development of a screenplay, writers nearly always need to produce supporting documents such as outlines, step outlines and treatments. Sometimes these are used as selling tools, where the writer shows producers a condensed version of the story to see if they're interested in buying or reading the script. Sometimes they're used as working documents, to help writers, script editors and producers stand back from the script and see the bigger picture of what they're trying to develop.

Writers sometimes have a fraught relationship with such development documents, seeing them as mechanical, dry and irrelevant, and a threat to the organic creative process. But they're essential tools to master if attending script meetings and securing commissions are going to be part of your screenwriting life.

The exercises in this chapter offer a variety of simple yet powerful ways to create such documents. They can be a saving grace during re-writing, too, when it becomes difficult to keep an objective overview and work out what the real story problems are. Working with the skeleton of a story lets writers get to the heart of the matter, and solve issues without being seduced by the details of dialogue or scene writing.

When referring to development documents, there are many similar terms that often cause confusion. Different people in the industry use the same term to mean different things, but these are the definitions used in this book:

Outline (or story outline): a short document, usually of one to three pages, telling the story in its entirety, in polished powerful prose with relevant feeling and tone. This can also be used as a pitching document.

Step outline: a bare-bones document, long or short, mapping out the story in separate units or scenes. It gives very brief descriptions of each major event, change or emotion (both inner and outer story). It's only used as a working document, never for pitching. It's sometimes also called a *beat sheet* or a *scene-by-scene.*

Sequence outline: a one- or two-page document giving a condensed overview of the complete story, breaking it down into eight sequences, where each sequence is described in a short paragraph. This is mainly used for features, and usually only as a working document.

Treatment: a comprehensive document telling the complete story in polished prose. A treatment is a longer version of a story outline, giving more detail. It can be anything from five to thirty-five pages, depending on what the producer wants and what the writer needs. It's used both as a working document and sometimes for pitching purposes.

Synopsis: a short prose piece summarising the story. It tends to be quite neutral and matter of fact, often written by someone other than the writer. It's not used as a working document or pitch, but rather for script reports (coverage) or reviews.

Working with outlines is similar to understanding the purpose of pitching. Here, writers can't lie to themselves, but are forced to look at the story the way it is, rather than what they think it is or want it to be. Working with outlines as a development tool means both initial creation and later rewriting can become more effective and enjoyable.

Power punch

If you have a full-length feature script and want to create a selling outline, it can feel difficult to condense all the information on to one short page. But instead of feeling as if you're losing the hard-earned richness, think of it as a taster that will entice readers to want more.

As with pitching, writing an outline is about capturing the essence of a story. Whether traditional or unconventional, by focusing on key events and moments, the core of the story will reveal itself. Sometimes it's more important to convey the feeling of the story rather than the facts. This exercise works with the concept of turning points; to read more about them, see 'All Change' in Chapter 6.

➢ Locate eight to ten main turning points in your story. These are moments when everything changes and things can no longer stay the same. It may be an event, reaction, insight or decision.

➢ For each turning point, create a 'power phrase' that really sums up what it's about. Try to move beyond the factual and into more emotional territory.

➢ Combine the power phrases into the best order. Read the story they form.

➢ Use this as the basis for your one-page outline. You may need to add information or find ways to bridge one phrase with another, but they offer a foundation of vibrant moments to build from.

For instance, if the turning point is:

> *Gupta realises the organisation he works for is corrupt and decides to blow the whistle*

possible power phrases could be:

○ *Who stands by and watches while people get hurt?*

○ *David and Goliath power-play.*

○ *A dangerous move makes the heart strong.*

There are many ways of finding phrases that resonate and ring true. When working with your story, allow yourself to try different possibilities until you find ones that sound good. There's no right or wrong, only ways to find potent words that help bring the story alive.

Mapping it out

Sequence outlines are an excellent tool both for building narrative and troubleshooting. They are especially useful for longer formats such as the feature, where it's easy to lose the plot and go off on tangents. They help provide clarity about the function of each section and how these combine and affect each other.

A sequence outline can be used even if the story doesn't have a classical three-act structure. In fact, it's particularly useful when working with unconventional structures, as it's then even more crucial to have a sense of the overarching form and how it relates to the content.

There are different models of how many sequences a feature has, but this exercise works with eight. Their main purpose is to give a clear overview of both content and connections, and help create clarity, focus and depth of meaning. Often they also reveal where there's not enough story or drive to sustain a feature.

➤ Choose a story you're working on and divide it into eight sequences. Write a short paragraph of what happens in each section.

➤ Read the paragraphs and try to find the focus of each sequence. What's it really about? What's the main question or drive in each sequence? What is it that unites all the events in that sequence?

➤ Write a short heading for each sequence, summing up the essence of what it's mainly about, both dramatically and thematically. For instance, a series of sequence headings could be:

Sequence 1: Leaving home.

Sequence 2: Finding new friends.

Sequence 3: Betrayal – no one knows who she really is.

Sequence 4: Lost and alone, deciding it's all too much.

Sequence 5: Entering a new world – new rules, new personality.

Sequence 6: Planning revenge, gathering strength.

Sequence 7: Taking back your life, but finding it no longer fits.

Sequence 8: Realising who your true friends are and what home means.

➤ Look at your story again and see if the scenes in each section relate to its sequence heading. Is this what they're really about? Do they come in the right place? What other things can happen to tell the story beat of the sequence heading? How do the scenes in a sequence build and function together? Rewrite your story, one sequence at a time, incorporating your new ideas.

A sequence heading functions as a guiding compass to the scenes in that section. It helps create coherence and deep structure, so that every part is in its right place and serves the whole. This can create comedy, emotion or suspense, reveal the best places for plants and pay-offs, and build subtle narrative that develops in a powerful way.

More than anything it creates focus on a deep level, so the story can move in unexpected exciting ways and still keep the central idea in place. It provides the overview so often missing from a writer's understanding of what they're doing. If this feels too systematic, don't worry. The scenes will create the complexity and detail, while being supported by a strong purposeful structure. It's a highly recommended tool that can improve scripts hugely with only a small amount of work.

Step to the beat

When writing a step outline, what you're essentially doing is laying out the dramatic beats in an order you think works, so that you'll have a strong overview of the whole. This will allow you to play around with the structure and orchestrate the most effective screenplay possible. Because it's more of a planning document than a pitching document, you can tailor it to what works best for you, in a style that pleases you. For example, some writers prefer to write the beats in simple concise sentences, whereas others prefer to expand the language so it becomes almost a hybrid treatment. Whichever way you prefer, the core purpose remains the same: to map out the physical and emotional beats of the screenplay, so that you can clearly see where the story's heading and, if necessary, shift the structure around to improve it.

The beauty of a step outline is that because writers lay down the beats under scene headings it can then be built up into a screenplay, rather than having to cross-reference different documents. In this way, a completed step outline provides a skeleton of the whole screenplay into which screen directions and dialogue can be written. It also means that if you're writing the screenplay out of order, you know what comes directly before and directly after, and can write those sequences with knowledge of exactly where they sit.

> ➤ For this exercise, you'll need to watch a short film of approximately ten minutes (there are specific websites and DVDs that showcase short films, or you may know someone who's made one). Try to make it a short film that you don't know well – one you're not close to.

➢ Watch the film a couple of times then construct a step outline for it. List all the scenes (INT. BAR – NIGHT, etc.) from beginning to end. Capture them all as there may be an important beat in even the most minor of scenes.

➢ Under each scene heading, describe what happens. Don't worry yet about specific beats; just write what you see and feel. You might need to watch the film a few times to capture everything.

➢ Now look at the description you've written and strip away any super-fluous information, keeping a clear sense of what the dramatic beats are, physical and emotional. Look beneath the surface to grasp what the scenes are trying to achieve. Remember that there may be multiple beats in a scene.

➢ When you're left with the bare bones of the story, see if you can summarise the beats of each scene in a sentence. Make it clear which are physical beats and which emotional. Go over the document a few times to really hone in on what's happening, and how the beats build on each other as the story progresses.

➢ What you're left with is a step outline. You've boiled down the whole film into a document that lays down the film's intentions to its reader, and guides them on a journey of experiencing the story through a written structural plan.

When you embark on your next screenplay, start by writing a step outline. Build it up by thinking carefully about the beats needed for your story, both physical and emotional. As you compile the beats, plotting the character's arc moment by moment, experiment with the structure to see what effect a different order might have. Writing a step outline isn't a quick and easy task, but it is one well worth undertaking before you embark on writing the actual screenplay. It can also be an invaluable tool during later stages of rewriting.

Bridge building

When summarising a story, it's often easy to get lost in the myriad of events and plot strands. Whether writing a short outline or long treat-ment, it helps to break it down into basic building blocks. But these pieces also have to connect – the story has to flow and make sense. Sometimes when a story's broken down into segments the writer knows how they relate, but the reader doesn't. This exercise will help you create more cohesion in your outlines.

➤ Choose a story you're working on. Write 150 words describing its beginning. Then write 150 words describing its ending.

➤ Now look at how to best connect the beginning and ending. Bullet-point the essential steps you need from the script, so the story makes sense. From this list, write 200 to 300 words that describe the middle.

➤ Now find three or four bridging moments that will move the beginning into the middle, then towards the end, creating a continuous flow. Think of what connects each step to the next.

➤ Put the beginning, middle and end descriptions together with the bridging moments, making sure they flow into one another. See how the story reads and polish as needed.

➤ If you're writing a long treatment, first create a sequence outline (see 'Mapping it Out'), then do the above exercise describing all its sequences, not just beginning, middle and end. Give yourself 500 words to describe each sequence and put them together, making sure they connect and make sense as a continuous flow.

This approach works with both classic and unconventional story structures. You don't need to know the acts, turning points or arcs. Just describe the building blocks of the story and allow a clear coherent picture to emerge in which they connect and flow.

Warm up workout

As with pitching, it's very useful to practise creating outlines from stories that are not your own. You'll be less wedded to them and more able to get an overview. If you find writing outlines hard, this is a good exercise to do on a regular basis, getting a feel for how to encapsulate a story without losing its essence, and how to use rhythm, mood and vocabulary to make the most of a limited word count.

➤ Choose a feature film you've seen and know well. Watch it again if you can. Try to summarise the story in one page, no more. Use rhythm and tone to make it readable and polished. Don't cram words into every space, use paragraph breaks and allow the story to breathe. Capture the bigger picture, rather than every detail.

> ➢ What's most important to include? What is the character journey, the crucial plot points, the theme? Include beginning, middle and end to tell a short punchy version of the complete story.

If you're new to writing screenplay outlines, or find them hard, do this exercise at least ten times over a couple of months to dedicate yourself to improving this crucial skill.

Subsuming subplots

Though you may know what the essential journey of your story is, there may also be one or two key subplots that need including. The danger with subplots is that there isn't enough space to explain them properly, so often they create more confusion than interest.

When writing a short outline, you have to accept there are many things that aren't going to be told right now. But if the outline is well written it can open the door for the full script to be read. If you do decide that a subplot must be included, aim to do it in such a way that it will really add to the outline rather than detract from it.

➢ To decide whether, and how, to include subplot information in a short outline, ask the following questions of each subplot strand in your story:

   ○ What's the essence of this subplot? What's its most important event?

   ○ How is the subplot related to the main plot? How does it affect the main story? What's its dramatic function? What's its thematic function?

   ○ How can you sum up the subplot in a single sentence?

   ○ Where in the outline is the most suitable place to declare it?

   ○ What happens to the outline if it's not included? Try it and see if the outline works without it.

➢ Practise telling your story verbally with the subplot information you feel is necessary. Ask the listener for feedback – what they found clear or confusing and whether they felt the subplot information a vital part of the story. Then tell it again without the subplot information, and compare the response.

Purple prose

A selling outline or treatment is meant to be an emotional experience for the reader. It's a condensed version of the story, not a dry summarising of facts. It needs to take the reader on a ride and make them feel: sadness, hope, joy, fear, sympathy, interest. Sometimes writers are so afraid of coming across as sentimental that they strip away too much emotion from their outlines; but this is unlikely to inspire or excite a reader. The treatment should touch people, affect them, so they won't be able to stop thinking about it.

A good treatment doesn't only tell the right story, it tells it in the right way. If it's a thriller, it must be thrilling. If it's a comedy, it must be funny. If it's a drama, it must be moving. You can't simply say it'll be funny, you have to make it funny. 'Show, don't tell' applies just as much to writing treatments as it does to scripts. Use all your skills as a writer when creating the selling documents. Write in the present tense, don't forget narrative perspective and point of view, and above all, craft the text so it carries the magic. This exercise will help you play with words and think about how to use them to paint a picture.

➢ Write a one- or two-page outline of your story (use the 'Bridge Building' exercise if needed).

➢ Rewrite it with as much 'purple prose' as you can – really ride the highs, plummet the depths. Allow over-the-top words and phrases to describe the drama. Let it be totally emotional, super-evocative and dangerously exciting; allow it all to come out and enjoy yourself!

➢ Read through and highlight places where you see something useful, a seed or a turn of phrase. Tone it down as necessary so it feels real and serious, but keep the emotion and drama alive. Where's the boundary? Where do you feel uncomfortable? What makes it real? What makes it moving? What makes it engaging? What do you want to keep?

➢ Take the initial outline and rewrite it three more times, each one feeling like a different genre – first drama, then comedy, then thriller. Keep to the same story and events, but change the way you describe them, using tone, vocabulary and rhythm as necessary.

➢ See how each of the three feels to read. What are the differences they create in the readerly experience? What makes them funny or exciting or touching? Can you apply these insights to improve the original outline?

Title and genre

Titles are very much about audience expectation. They create an image and an emotional desire that correlates with the promise of a certain type of story shape or character journey. If you're writing in a specific genre, it's crucial to spend time developing a title that evokes the right response in the audience. Producers need to think about audience figures and money, so a good title can really help to sell your idea in just a few words.

➢ Look at the following potential film titles and write a sentence about what kind of film you'd expect from each. Describe the genre and type of story you'd expect, and also the type of protagonist. Is there a way you can improve the title?

○ *Fly Away Peter, Fly Away Paul*

○ *The Prediction*

○ *Who's There?*

○ *The Coach*

○ *When All Seems Lost . . .*

○ *Mrs Bradley Has a Plan*

○ *Say Goodbye, Little Laura*

➢ Look at the titles of your own screenplays and think about what they might suggest to an audience. Do they capture the genre? Do they promise a certain type of story and protagonist? Does the rhythm of the title sound appropriate? Have similar titles been used elsewhere? If so, are they of the same genre? Which colours does your title evoke, and do they relate to a particular tone? Why would someone want to see a film or TV drama with your title?

Naming the game

You may feel you already know the right title of your script, but it's always useful to explore other possibilities. The title is the very first meeting between film and audience. It needs to fulfil a number of functions: suggest theme or story, create interest, express tone, fit the genre. A good title can also deepen the audience's understanding of the subtext and theme once they've seen the film.

The creative screenwriter

➢ Read the story below.

> *Lin and Yusuf run a small museum of sacred artefacts. They're passionate*
> *and work hard. But unknown to them, boss Paula's got into financial*
> *trouble and been persuaded by a property company to sell the land*
> *around the museum. The museum can stay but will be turned into a*
> *commercial circus. Either Lin or Yusuf will lose their job, as only one can*
> *stay. In protest, Lin hands in her notice and urges Yusuf to do the same.*
> *Yusuf feels he can do more good from the inside and stays on. He tries*
> *to persuade Paula to stop the sale, but to no avail. On the day the*
> *digging starts, Lin's friends mount a large sit-in protest. During the*
> *mayhem, Lin breaks into the museum and steals the artefacts, feeling*
> *they're no longer properly cared for. Yusuf discovers her, and feels he*
> *must tell the police. Lin drops the artefact and it breaks. Inside is an old*
> *photograph of the family it originated from. Observing it, Yusuf realises*
> *he's forgotten that he does this work to keep stories of the past alive.*
> *Yusuf and Lin join forces and legally free the artefacts. They set up a*
> *travelling museum that brings the artefacts back to their people,*
> *helping them to reconnect with their forgotten histories and legacies.*

➢ Free-associate a list of words or phrases that come to you while
  reading the story.

➢ Look at your list and highlight ones that feel special in some way.
  From these, brainstorm ten possible titles for the story.

➢ Choose your favourite three, and consider what each one offers in
  terms of theme, tone, genre and audience expectations. Which would
  you choose as the most fitting title, and why?

17

Discovering
voice

A writer's individual voice can be hard to define, especially when they have to contemplate their own work. At the same time, it's very much part of what makes a writer special and, to some degree, successful. The very idea of a 'writing voice' can refer to many things: the kind of ideas a writer has, the way their stories are told, or a certain tone in dialogue or scene writing. A writer's voice is also something delicate. If you come at it like a bull in a china shop, it can wilt and die. If you're too aware of it and become self-conscious, the magic disappears and what was once a natural voice can feel staged and over-rehearsed.

So why is it useful for a writer to know about their voice? One answer is that it gives a sense of what makes you memorable as a writer. It helps you see what types of stories you want to tell, and what types of stories you're best able to tell (these aren't always the same, sadly). It means that when you get the opportunity to work with producers, you're aware of what you can offer and if your voice will fit what they're looking for. You can value the things you're good at, and accept the ones you're not. This becomes especially important in long-running TV series, where producers look for a variety of voices that suit the overall tone of the show yet also have distinct qualities. For some writers, it can be a real challenge to fit their voice into an already established story world.

Understanding your own voice isn't about setting it in stone. It's about discovering who you are as a writer, and making the most of it.

This can bring strength and confidence so that, rather than trying to emulate others, you trust your own voice and what it is that makes it specific and personal. Every writer has something unique, and the more you can identify this the better chance you'll have of standing out from the crowd and getting producers to commission your work. What's also important to remember is that as you develop and grow as a person, so does your voice. As you become interested and experienced in different things, and your perspective matures and morphs, so does your writing style. This, again, is something to be embraced.

Discovering a voice can also help writers to find the most suitable area in which to work in the business. A voice might best belong in TV series writing, where there's more room to work with characters over a longer period of time; a writer might have a flair for children's stories, and come to specialise in work for that particular audience; or a writer who is a hopelessly sentimental cynic, with a fascinating and funny take on the world, might work well in big-screen comedy. All these qualities can become gold dust if they're respected and nurtured.

This chapter, then, tries to tiptoe ever so gently around your voice, to hear what it might be telling you. You don't need to look it too much in the face, or keep too much control over it. In fact, when you think you know all about it, then maybe it's time to let go and try something new. You don't want your voice to become stale or laboured; give it room to grow. It's simply about having a sense of it, and then once you know yourself better as a writer, cast off again and forget about it. If you try and force it, and try constantly to write in a particular voice rather than simply write, it almost never works.

A matter of style

It's not only ideas that distinguish a writer. It's how they're expressed, and the way they're explored through a story. This is a particularly important feature when working with producers, who want to know why they should commission you instead of one of the many other writers available to them.

➢ This exercise needs to be done with three to five writers. It can be done physically together, or virtually by email or internet. The important thing is that you all do the same exercise and exchange it with one another.

➢ Choose one of the three premises below. Make sure that all writers taking part use the same premise. Every writer should write a one- to two-page outline of the story as they imagine it. All writers should keep the essential ingredients of the premise, but beyond this there's much that can be added, including an ending.

○ *Dora and Carmen discover a secret bank vault and begin to lead a life of luxury, doing all the things they always wanted to.*

○ *Deepak longs to play the most beautiful music in the world, and makes a dangerous journey to discover its source.*

○ *A new vaccine against laziness has been discovered. All the world's couch potatoes are being rounded up and treated . . . whether they like it or not.*

➢ Once you've written your outlines, share them with each other so that every person reads every outline. Think about how the various stories written from the same premise differ. What makes each special? What are the hallmarks? Is it to do with ideas, plot, type of characters or a certain tone? What perspective is offered on the story? What makes each writer's voice distinct, and how is this revealed?

➢ Share your thoughts with each other. Read what the other writers reveal about your, and your story's, voice. Does it ring true with you? Or do you see something else as typical of your voice? If so, why might this not be coming through?

Patchwork quilt

Finding your voice is often more of a reflective endeavour than an active one. It's not possible to decide what voice you have, then set off and write according to plan. Instead, the voice reveals itself, slowly and gradually, like the sea eating into granite and honing shapes. Sometimes it's easier to discover your voice by looking at the work you've already created.

➢ Take five outlines or screenplays that you've written (or ten if you have them). Look at them one at a time, and ask:

○ What's most important to me in this story?

○ Why did I want to write it?

     o What do I most like in it?

     o What is its hidden part?

     o How will it reach the world and its audience?

➤ Read through all your answers to one question at a time. What do you find by seeing them together, laid out like a patchwork quilt? What's revealed about you and your writing? What overall picture emerges about the type of thing you naturally seem to write?

➤ From this, try to describe your writing voice in one or two sentences. Use your intuition rather than thinking hard about it. Be playful, lyrical, evocative, engaging. When you read this description of your voice, how does it feel?

Treasure chest

All writers have a unique life that makes them special. It may not seem spectacular, but it's yours, and the only one you have. What's important is to unlock this treasure chest so that the stories within it can be found. These are the ideas that no one else could have, and they form the foundation of who you are as a writer.

At the same time, all your stories aren't ones that should necessarily be told to the world. Some of them may be, some of them not. But they're stories that matter to you, and as such they inform and shape your writing voice.

➤ Write a piece of free prose, as long as you want, about:

     o The first memory you have of life.

     o The thing you most remember about school.

     o Your first kiss.

     o How you knew you were an adult.

     o An important trip you made.

     o The thing you most miss in the world.

➤ Read through what you've written. With each piece, think about what most strikes you. Is it a tone, a moment, an image, a person? What in this memory fragment do you think could become a story?

➢ Create a character and give them a name. Now put that character into one of your fragments and allow the character to talk about it, as if it happened to them. What do they tell you? Does it change? Is there something that interests you in it? How could it be developed further?

This exercise isn't about autobiography or creating stories from life. It's more about hearing the personal stories that make you who you are, and allowing them to fertilise your writing in whatever way they need. You may never write any of them into a script, but telling them to yourself may make you a better writer.

Harmonising voices

Some screenwriters write in pairs or teams, and although this might dilute an individual's voice it can also create an original, exciting and marketable combined writing voice. Beyond the practicality of ensuring that the writers can work together and respect each other's contributions, comes the wonderful opportunity of harmonising individual voices into a collective tone. This works especially well in comedy or television, where writers can spark off one another to tell jokes or create complex sets of characters, but it can also work in short films and features. Whatever the format, if you're co-writing it's important to spend time getting to know each other's style and writing approach so a common language can be agreed on and used.

➢ For this exercise, work with either a partner or a small group. If you're working in a group, limit it to a maximum of four people.

➢ Read the following premise and each write a 500-word monologue responding to the immediate situation from the character's perspective. You don't have to limit the monologue to talking about the situation, but it should stem from it.

> *Captain Jack Ellis is an experienced airline pilot. He's been working in the industry for over thirty years and is well respected. He's known for being a great mentor to new pilots. One day, on a flight to Auckland, an emergency warning signal comes up. He's experienced things like this before, but none of them have ever come to anything serious. Today, though, for some unknown reason he suddenly panics.*

➢ Each person should read out their monologue in turn, then analyse each other's. What did you like about their monologue? What perspective did it take? How did it develop, structurally? What did it refer to beyond the immediate situation? How effective was it? What was good about the language and tone? What didn't you like about it, and why? If you had to rewrite it, what would you do? How would you try to keep as much of the original as possible, but improve on it?

➢ Pick out elements from each monologue that you like and you think could work well together. Bring them all together and find a voice for Jack that incorporates everyone's ideas. Each write one final monologue in this harmonised voice. Refine it until everyone's happy, then consider the final voice. How similar or different is it from your personal voice? Do you think it's stronger now? How do you feel about writing in this style? How do you feel about writing in this team?

Hand in hand

If you're employed on a TV series, writing adaptations, or taking on script commissions, you might sometimes feel a tension between what you'd like to write and what the producer wants. It can be a tricky balancing act between giving them what they're expecting and writing what you feel the project needs. It's useful to remember that most of the time you'll have been selected for the job not only for your technical ability as a screenwriter, but also for your style, ideas and previous body of work. So even when writing to order, bringing your individual voice to a project is a crucial aspect of the work. The essential element here is to discover the complementary connections between your voice and that belonging to characters and story worlds that have been invented by other people.

➢ Read this commission brief and answer the questions that follow it:

Coping with Hayden *is a six-part TV drama series that shows Mr and Mrs Simpkins being forced to accept their adult son back into the family fold. Hayden's now forty, but after losing his job and all his money through gambling, he's got no choice except to return home. What Hayden doesn't realise is that since he left twenty years ago his parents have decided to lead separate lives and opt for an open relationship.*

o What interests you most about this world?

o What resonates with you about the various characters' situations?

- What plot lines would you enjoy seeing them in?

- What additional characters would you like to create?

- Find one thing you really care about in this premise.

- What specific writing strengths and skills could you bring to the project?

- What connection can you find between your voice and the series theme?

- Why would you be a good a writer to work on this series?

Even though the brief might not appeal to you instantly, think hard about what *you* could bring to it that other writers couldn't. Such work is part of living and working as a professional screenwriter, and finding a way to fuse your voice with the tone of the story and the vision of the producer can be exciting, surprising and rewarding.

Hidden resources

After a few years' experience, whether writing professionally or for your own pleasure, you build up writing patterns, skills and resources. We all employ different creative processes, and these can be a great help as we realise we often know more than we think. But even the best writers regularly experience problems. When something troubling happens it's not always a sign that the writer's doing something wrong, but can simply be part of the everyday reality of being a writer. However, the manner in which you deal with problems determines the outcome and whether it can be turned to an advantage. How you react to difficulties during the script development process is also part of your writing voice and persona, and can be defined and developed.

➢ Think about the hardest writing problem you've faced and managed to solve. How did you do it? What helped you find the answer? What makes you happy about the way you dealt with the problem?

➢ Now think about another writing problem whose outcome you don't feel satisfied with. What made it difficult? What stopped you from reaching a solution? Have you faced similar issues during other script projects? Does this tell you anything useful about your individual writing process?

➢ Reflect on how you as a writer tend to deal with problems. How do they make you feel? How do you react to them? Are there other ways to face them? How would you like to deal with them? What can you learn from problems when they come?

➢ Write 500 words on how problems could help you to tell your stories: what are you good at dealing with in writing problems? What do you want to develop further? What do you need to remember when faced with a new writing problem?

The joy of writing

It may have been forgotten after years of hard work, but at some point in their life every writer decided to write because they enjoyed it. Personal reasons for writing are thus also part of what kind of writer someone is, and remembering what's important can provide a writer with resilience and motivation in times of creative struggle or drought.

Most of the time, no one apart from the writer would be too disappointed if they didn't actually write. Essentially it happens because the writer wants to do it; no one's forcing or imploring them. If success or money are the main driving factors, in the end they'll only take you so far. There has to be a connection to wanting to communicate and to express something from inside you. Defining this personal relationship to your writing and why you do it can help to strengthen your creative voice, fostering stamina, belief and enthusiasm.

➢ Put all pens, paper and computers away and go out for a walk. As you move, look around you and allow yourself to relax. Begin to muse and reflect on why you write, and what originally drove you to it. Keep walking and consider what you most love about writing – not just what you thought would be good about it back when you started, but how you feel about it right now, today. Where's your joy in writing? When do you feel it? How is it expressed? How does it feel now as you're walking? What connects you back to it?

➢ When you come back from the walk, write a love letter to Writing. Tell it all the things you really adore about it; all the ways it brings you joy; why you don't want to live without it. Enjoy the letter as you write it! Express it in any way you want; have fun, play, be surprising, heartfelt, honest, and real.

> ➤ Read the letter aloud to yourself and see how it makes you feel. Summarise the letter into a single sentence, beginning with: *I really love writing because . . .*

> ➤ Write this sentence on a card and place it by your computer or in your notebook. Put the letter in a safe place and take it out to read whenever you need to. Repeat this exercise as much as you want, preferably once a year, or when your writing feels difficult.

The writer's life

As your life changes, so will your writing tastes and writing needs. You go through new experiences and want to write about them; you begin to appreciate different emotional values and see situations from different perspectives; or you simply crave to step out of your comfort zone and try something fresh and exciting. Whatever changes in you will spill over into your writing and affect your voice. This isn't something to be afraid of – in fact, it should be celebrated. After all, writing is about telling the stories you want to tell and sharing your views of the world. Changing your voice as you develop means that you're growing as a writer, and it's a good idea to be aware of this so you can make the most of it.

> ➤ Write five ideas that you'd like to develop into screenplays right now. Choose only those you feel strongly about, and really want to tell to the world. They don't need to be ready-formed stories, simply kernels of ideas.

> ➤ Look at the first script you ever wrote. What was the story about? What was it you really cared about in the story? Why was it important to you? Why did you choose to write this particular story? Try to summarise your response in one or two sentences.

> ➤ Compare your five current ideas with your first script. Do you see any connections between them in terms of voice, style, tone or theme? Have these features evolved in any way, or have they disappeared and been replaced with new ones? What kind of writer would you say you were at the beginning, and what kind of writer would you say you are now? Write 500 words to describe yourself as a writer to yourself, using your innermost, heartfelt thoughts, without trying to promote or emphasise your talents.

The creative screenwriter

> ➤ If you've been writing for some time, it's a good idea to add a third stage where you examine scripts you wrote a couple of years ago to see how they compare with your first stories and those you want to write now. What's similar and different about your tone, genres, themes and characters? What stories have been successful? What scripts were never completed? How does knowing what worked and what didn't work build an understanding of your past and present writing voice?

> ➤ Do this exercise again in a year's time, and revisit the list of ideas you wanted to tell today. If you haven't already done so, do you still yearn to write them? Are they still important to you? Do you see something different in them that you'd now prefer to explore? How do you think you've moved on as a writer in the year, both in terms of ideas and writing skill?

Conclusion

DIY SCRIPT SURGERY

The exercises in this book can be used in any way you want and need. You can work through them from beginning to end; dip into special sections to improve your craft; or use them as an aid to enhance projects you're already working on. What's important is to engage in regular creative writing practice, where you enhance skills, techniques, ideas and imagination on an ongoing basis, rather than only when writing actual screenplays.

Getting into the habit of working with freestanding exercises will help you warm up, increase your productivity and flow, and enhance your problem solving abilities. However, even with an established creative routine, screenwriters can encounter the common ailments of the trade. This can be debilitating and painful; the muse deserts you and you forget everything you know, stuck in a hole with no way out. In fact, it's not necessarily evidence of doing something wrong, but sometimes simply a natural part of the screenwriting process.

To help you become even more creative, exciting and effective as a screenwriter, we'd like to conclude by offering a series of tailor-made work plans that'll help you collect creative solutions and confidence, even when the going gets tough. This DIY Script Surgery should help kick-start you when you feel stranded, expand and exercise your creative thinking, and address persistent predicaments that keep your writing from being as good as it should be.

Below, we highlight a series of afflictions you may experience as a screenwriter. At some point in your career, you're likely to encounter most of them. For each, a set of exercises have been gathered from the various chapters, and prescribed as treatment. You can of course pick your own path through the book or simply work through a particular chapter, but when you feel low, uninspired or uncertain, these work plans are a great aid in getting back on track. You may also at times receive professional feedback that pinpoints specific weaknesses in a script, which you then want to focus on in the next draft. Facing up to these problem areas can feel like torture, but it's good to be honest about what you need to do to improve your story.

This final section is like a personalised training programme at the writing gym, helping you tackle pernicious problem areas. The recommended exercises aren't always the obvious ones, but have been selected to complement each other and create a beneficial exercise regime that'll tackle the given issue from various angles, with various methods, to better help you break through the difficulty you find yourself in.

So, here we present further possible routes through the book; creative medicine for those times when you're in need of extra help or inspiration.

DIAGNOSES AND RECOMMENDED REMEDIES

Writer's block

You can't seem to think of anything to write. You feel stuck and as if you've dried up. You feel like a terrible writer and just want to give up. Every time you try to force an idea, it gets worse. You become disconnected and afraid. This can be particularly terrifying when working to a deadline, when you know you have to produce something good – and fast!

PRESCRIPTION

Undertake at least one a day, for two weeks, or until you feel better:

All exercises from Chapter 1
Into the unknown (Chapter 2)
In the news (Chapter 2)
What's around you? (Chapter 2)
Dot to dot (Chapter 3)
One thing leads to another (Chapter 3)
Back to the future (Chapter 3)
Character building (Chapter 4)
What's in a name? (Chapter 4)
A matter of perspective (Chapter 5)
Listening out for relationships (Chapter 5)
Chain reaction (Chapter 6)
Making things worse (Chapter 6)
Alternative routes (Chapter 7)

Mix it up (Chapter 7)
One step beyond (Chapter 8)
Damp squib (Chapter 8)
A whole new world (Chapter 9)
Bricks and mortar (Chapter 9)
Location, location, location (Chapter 9)
Home sweet home (Chapter 10)
Turn up the heat (Chapter 11)
Valued objects (Chapter 12)
Say what you see (Chapter 12)
Silent talk (Chapter 13)
Lying and denying (Chapter 13)
Reigniting the spark (Chapter 14)
Give yourself a break (Chapter 14)
Warm up workout (Chapter 16)
The joy of writing (Chapter 17)

Uninspiring ideas

Your ideas are fine but sometimes feel a little obvious, over-familiar or flat. They work, but there are no great surprises. Sometimes you're even bored with them yourself. You may be too comfortable with your writing, stuck in a groove where you always end up with the same old characters or plot solutions. You're not really using all your abilities and skills, but taking the easy way out, accepting the first thing that presents itself and feeling relieved you don't have to do more work.

PRESCRIPTION

Limiting yourself (Chapter 1)
Listening to an onion (Chapter 1)
Having fun (Chapter 1)
Wordplay (Chapter 1)
All exercises from Chapter 2
All exercises from Chapter 3
Pinpointing the protagonist (Chapter 4)
A creative portrait (Chapter 4)
Character building (Chapter 4)
The odd couple (Chapter 5)
Absent friends (Chapter 5)
Inciting incidents (Chapter 6)

All change (Chapter 6)
Alternative routes (Chapter 7)
Where are you going? (Chapter 7)
Multiple protagonists (Chapter 7)
Parallel stories (Chapter 7)
Shapeshifting (Chapter 7)
First impressions (Chapter 8)
Beyond the sea (Chapter 9)
When are we? (Chapter 9)
Opening doors (Chapter 9)
Mix and match (Chapter 10)
The telling moment (Chapter 11)
Compare and contrast (Chapter 12)
Rhythm and tempo (Chapter 14)
A matter of style (Chapter 17)

Sketchy characters

Your characters feel like characters rather than human beings. They're one-sided or too simplistic. They may not be interesting enough to an audience, or able to carry the story to the end. They need to provide more fuel, and fit the theme better. You may only have explored the most obvious side of them, without looking deeper. If you're honest, you may even be most interested in your characters as pawns for the plot and want them to simply do your bidding, without hearing their side of the story or allowing them to complicate matters.

PRESCRIPTION

Magic moments (Chapter 1)
What do you know? What don't you know? (Chapter 2)
Bringing people together (Chapter 2)
Conflict vs meaningful conflict (Chapter 3)
Planning the plan (Chapter 3)
All exercises from Chapter 4
All exercises from Chapter 5
Character arc as structure (Chapter 6)
Deepening the problem (Chapter 6)
Pain and problems (Chapter 8)
Outside the comfort zone (Chapter 9)
A common language (Chapter 9)

Genre protagonists (Chapter 10)
Swap shop (Chapter 12)
Valued objects (Chapter 12)
Imprisoned (Chapter 12)
All exercises from Chapter 13
Collapsible cast (Chapter 14)
Treasure chest (Chapter 17)

Insufficient plot

Your idea and characters work, but there's not enough going on. The story gets repetitive towards the middle and you're not sure where to go next. The things that happen may feel too obvious, disjointed, unclear or not dramatic enough. Events are not related to the theme as you lose the plot and no longer keep focused on what you want to say and how it all fits together. You need more twists, turns and complications to make the story come alive and fulfil its promise.

PRESCRIPTION

Ready, steady, go! (Chapter 1)
Creative collisions (Chapter 2)
Trading places (Chapter 2)
Plotting a story (Chapter 3)
What's the problem? (Chapter 3)
What happens next? (Chapter 3)
Inside out (Chapter 4)
Stepping into change (Chapter 4)
Motivating action (Chapter 4)
Antagonist as thematic driver (Chapter 5)
The third party (Chapter 5)
Weaving webs (Chapter 5)
Planning the plan (Chapter 6)
Deepening the problem (Chapter 6)
Rising action (Chapter 6)
Making things worse (Chapter 6)
Chain reaction (Chapter 6)
Alternative routes (Chapter 7)
Outside the comfort zone (Chapter 9)
Playing by the rules (Chapter 9)
Mapping it out (Chapter 11)

Complicating factors (Chapter 11)
Turn up the heat (Chapter 11)
Valued objects (Chapter 12)
Trading spaces (Chapter 12)
Running out of fuel (Chapter 14)
Stuck in the mud (Chapter 14)
Mapping it out (Chapter 16)
Step to the beat (Chapter 16)

Unclear theme

There may be many interesting elements and good moments in your script. The surface plot works pretty well, but somehow it isn't making enough impact. The script isn't coming together and creating a strong, clear whole; it remains as disparate strands trying to connect and reach each other. You may not even be sure what it is you're really writing about or wanting to say. You may feel dazed and confused after receiving too much feedback from too many people, and need to find your own focus and rediscover the reason you're telling this story.

PRESCRIPTION

Finding your compass (Chapter 3)
Conflict vs meaningful conflict (Chapter 3)
Motivating action (Chapter 4)
Weaving webs (Chapter 5)
Finding the right antagonist (Chapter 5)
Structuring the emotional journey (Chapter 6)
Deepening the problem (Chapter 6)
Multiple protagonists (Chapter 7)
Telling the time (Chapter 7)
Shapeshifting (Chapter 7)
Setting the dramatic question (Chapter 8)
Mirror, mirror (Chapter 8)
Outside the comfort zone (Chapter 9)
Themes and dreams (Chapter 10)
Fulfilling the function (Chapter 11)
The telling moment (Chapter 11)
Compare and contrast (Chapter 12)
Key phrase (Chapter 13)
What's really going on? (Chapter 14)

Finding your focus (Chapter 15)
The question is . . . (Chapter 15)
Mapping it out (Chapter 16)
Naming the game (Chapter 16)

Credibility gaps

You may have a good idea, engaging characters and a plot with a solid structure, but some of the things that happen just aren't believable enough; they kind of fit, but lack depth and authenticity. Sometimes characters act out of character because you want them to fulfil a certain plot point. The rules of the world may not be clear enough, or aren't being complied with by the cast. There isn't enough reason or motivation for the characters' actions or reactions. The script feels like a made-up story rather than a real believable world.

PRESCRIPTION

Magic moments (Chapter 1)
Finding your compass (Chapter 3)
What's the problem? (Chapter 3)
Conflict vs meaningful conflict (Chapter 3)
Planning the plan (Chapter 3)
Back to the future (Chapter 3)
Character building (Chapter 4)
Inside out (Chapter 4)
Motivating action (Chapter 4)
Public and private spheres (Chapter 4)
Weaving webs (Chapter 5)
Family values (Chapter 5)
A matter of perspective (Chapter 5)
Listening out for relationships (Chapter 5)
Chain reaction (Chapter 6)
Planning the plan (Chapter 6)
Plants and payoffs (Chapter 6)
Essential facts (Chapter 8)
Full stop (Chapter 8)
Playing by the rules (Chapter 9)
Fitting the bill (Chapter 10)
Fulfilling the function (Chapter 11)
Scene structure (Chapter 11)

Show, don't tell (Chapter 12)
Speaking relations (Chapter 13)
Guess who (Chapter 13)
Creating a need to know (Chapter 13)
Stuck in the mud (Chapter 14)

Lacklustre prose

You have good ideas but your way of expressing them is fairly conventional, and could be more exciting. Your pitches and selling outlines are clear and functional, but don't set the world on fire. You choose obvious and familiar ways of phrasing your ideas instead of delving deeper into the way that words and sentences can conjure up magic. You may want to really move and touch people, but feel afraid of being too melodramatic or sentimental.

PRESCRIPTION

Limiting yourself (Chapter 1)
Listening to an onion (Chapter 1)
Being bad (Chapter 1)
Supermarket sweep (Chapter 4)
Listening out for relationships (Chapter 5)
Opening doors (Chapter 9)
Bricks and mortar (Chapter 9)
Inner worlds (Chapter 9)
Setting the mood (Chapter 10)
It's no joke (Chapter 10)
Topping and tailing (Chapter 11)
Crossing over (Chapter 11)
Doing, not being (Chapter 12)
Say what you see (Chapter 12)
I spy (Chapter 12)
Speaking relations (Chapter 13)
Talking in tongues (Chapter 13)
The voice of the world (Chapter 13)
Pitching the right note (Chapter 15)
Purple prose (Chapter 16)
Treasure chest (Chapter 17)
Harmonising voices (Chapter 17)

Never ending stories

You have no problem starting stories, but somewhere along the way you lose interest and jump ship to other ideas. Whatever you're working on, another project always feels more exciting. You've got piles of good scripts lying around, but none have been finished; at least not to a high enough standard to show. You may feel you're not really good enough as a writer, and worry about failure if you send your work out into the world.

PRESCRIPTION

Spontaneous storytelling (Chapter 1)
Being bad (Chapter 1)
Finding the plot, finding the emotion (Chapter 2)
One thing leads to another (Chapter 3)
Dot to dot (Chapter 3)
Stepping into change (Chapter 4)
Antagonist as thematic driver (Chapter 5)
Character arc as structure (Chapter 6)
Tying up loose ends (Chapter 6)
Full stop (Chapter 8)
Last dance (Chapter 8)
One step beyond (Chapter 8)
Damp squib (Chapter 8)
Temptations (Chapter 14)
Running out of fuel (Chapter 14)
Stuck in the mud (Chapter 14)
The heart of the matter (Chapter 15)
Finding your focus (Chapter 15)
Falling in love again (Chapter 15)
Mapping it out (Chapter 16)
Step to the beat (Chapter 16)
Warm up workout (Chapter 16)
Hidden resources (Chapter 17)

Sick and tired

Somewhere along the way you lost your enthusiasm for the project you're writing. You're bored with the story and its characters, and no longer care what happens to them. You may have been working on the script for a long time, or you may have got stuck recently and feel frustrated and angry with it for not performing in the way you want. Maybe you've just had some feedback that's left you unsure, unhappy or depressed. Whatever the disengagement, you need to reconnect and remember what the fire is that burns for you in the story.

PRESCRIPTION

Any exercise from Chapter 1
What do you know? What don't you know? (Chapter 2)
Losing the plot (Chapter 3)
Character building (Chapter 4)
A matter of perspective (Chapter 5)
All change (Chapter 6)
Making things worse (Chapter 6)
Alternative routes (Chapter 7)
Pains and problems (Chapter 8)
When are we? (Chapter 9)
Mix and match (Chapter 10)
The telling moment (Chapter 11)
Imprisoned (Chapter 12)
Through their eyes (Chapter 13)
Reigniting the spark (Chapter 14)
Give yourself a break (Chapter 14)
Power punch (Chapter 16)
The joy of writing (Chapter 17)

Final draft polish

You've done a lot of work on your screenplay, and reworked numerous drafts. You've put a lot of time and effort into finding your characters, focusing theme and honing structure. Most scenes are pretty effective and the general story's in good shape. You're happy and may feel done with it, but you also know that the final stage of polishing a draft one last time can work wonders and make a difference between a good and a great script. So, take a deep breath and prepare to dive into the screenplay one more time to make sure it's as good as it can possibly be.

PRESCRIPTION

Planning the plan (Chapter 3)
Public and private spheres (Chapter 4)
Absent friends (Chapter 5)
Rising action (Chapter 6)

Plants and payoffs (Chapter 6)
Mix it up (Chapter 7)
Starting over (Chapter 8)
Last dance (Chapter 8)
One step beyond (Chapter 8)
Location, location, location (Chapter 9)
Fitting the bill (Chapter 10)
All exercises from Chapter 11
All exercises from Chapter 12
All exercises from Chapter 13
Give yourself a break (Chapter 14)
Collapsible cast (Chapter 14)
The heart of the matter (Chapter 15)
Mapping it out (Chapter 16)

Selling your stories

You may be a good writer, but somehow don't have much luck selling your work. You keep writing, but your scripts don't take off. Your ideas are not as strong as they could be; your scripts may not be worked through to a high enough standard. You may not know what it is you're writing, or why. You know you want to be a writer, but aren't sure how to take the leap into the world where people want to listen to what you have to say.

PRESCRIPTION

Going to the heart (Chapter 2)
The hardest choice (Chapter 2)
Assessing story potential (Chapter 3)
Conflict vs meaningful conflict (Chapter 3)
Pinpointing the protagonist (Chapter 4)
Weaving webs (Chapter 5)
Character arc as structure (Chapter 6)
Deepening the problem (Chapter 6)
Shapeshifting (Chapter 7)
Reframing the familiar (Chapter 9)
Finding form (Chapter 10)
Fulfilling the function (Chapter 11)
All the exercises from Chapter 15
All the exercises from Chapter 16
Patchwork quilt (Chapter 17)

Treasure chest (Chapter 17)
Hand in hand (Chapter 17)
Hidden resources (Chapter 17)

And finally . . .

Committing to a regular creative practice, particularly when you feel it's demanding or you're under pressure, is one of the signs of a professional writer – someone who loves to write, and wants to be even better at it; someone who doesn't only expect their scripts to serve them with fame and fortune but who honestly feels that they serve their stories and want do their utmost to tell them well.

If you love to write and want to increase your creativity and improve your craft, this book grants you one extra bonus quality. Each chapter contains a number of suggested stories, ideas and premises. To really refine your artistry, pick one and write a script from it. If you do this once a month, you'll have an instant way of practising screenwriting where you don't have to worry about coming up with ideas. Instead, you can take what's already here and find a way to make it your own, and make it good. It's often when we work on other people's ideas or come away from the pressure of our own projects that the imagination relaxes and can really begin to flourish. In this way, producing practice pieces from ready-made ideas may also help to fertilise your own stories, as creative muscles come to life and start feeding an abundance of new ideas into any script you're working on.

We'd also like to stress the importance of working with the exercises in this book over time – not just completing them once, but finding ways to revisit them and make them part of your regular writing practice. You might find that by repeating an exercise, your understanding of it improves, and that every time you do it, something new comes from it. You may start to feel yourself 'stepping up' and achieving a better command of the more challenging exercises. This isn't something you ever complete. Improving as a screenwriter shouldn't be approached as a goal you achieve, but rather as a regular ongoing workout that helps keep you in constant good creative shape.

Work with this book in whichever way best suits you, and let the book work for you. As writers, script editors and teachers, we truly value the use of creative writing exercises as a way to improve screenwriting craft, and hope that through engaging with this book you'll start to feel this too and continue to produce ever better scripts. What else can we say but: write, imagine, be endlessly creative – and enjoy!